TALES FROM THE
PITTSBURGH PENGUINS
LOCKER ROOM

TALES FROM THE
PITTSBURGH PENGUINS
LOCKER ROOM

A COLLECTION OF THE GREATEST
PENGUINS STORIES EVER TOLD

JOE STARKEY

FOREWORD BY
MIKE LANGE

Sports Publishing books may be purchased in bulk at special discounts
for sales promotion, corporate gifts, fund-raising, or educational
purposes. Special editions can also be created to specifications. For
details, contact the Special Sales Department, Sports Publishing,
307 West 36th Street, 11th Floor, New York, NY 10018 or
sportspubbooks@skyhorsepublishing.com.

Sports Publishing® is a registered trademark of Skyhorse Publishing,
Inc.®, a Delaware corporation.

Visit our website at www.sportspubbooks.com.

10 9 8 7 6 5 4 3 2 1

Library of Congress Cataloging-in-Publication Data is available on file.

Cover design by Tom Lau
Cover photo credit: *Pittsburgh Tribune-Review*

ISBN: 978-1-68358-027-0
Ebook ISBN: 978-1-68358-036-2

Printed in the United States of America

TO MY FATHER, WHO INSTILLED
IN ME A LOVE OF STORIES.

CONTENTS

FOREWORD

Y ou'd have to be here to believe it: 50 years of Penguins hockey, 40-plus years of calling games, and 10 years since I wrote the foreword to the first edition of *Tales From the Pittsburgh Penguins Locker Room.*

And I'll tell you, this latest Stanley Cup run, the one you'll be reading about in the newest edition of this book, was really something special.

If you ask me how it was different, I'd say this: every single guy was a star. That was the impressive thing, to see how they played together. How they all had their moment. Nobody could pick an MVP. That lends credence to what I'm saying.

When I came along in 1974, the Penguins were not a major story. They were dealing with the Steelers, who were on their first Super Bowl run, and the Pirates, who were a dynamic team, and Pitt football, which was about to win a national championship. Our whole staff—coaching, marketing, everything—was about 12 people. Seriously. And after my first year, we went bankrupt.

The turning point was Ed DeBartolo taking control of the franchise in 1978. Without him, I don't think hockey survives in Pittsburgh. He put money into it until Mario arrived in 1984. Then the magic happened.

I've said this, and I honestly believe it: Mario is one of the luckiest people I've ever been around. Just something about him where things turn to gold.

My God, look at the people we've had through the years here. The Hall of Famers. The stars. Francis, Murphy, Mullen, Jagr, Barrasso, Bowman, Badger Bob, Recchi, Trottier, Stevens, Guerin, Gonchar, Coffey, Crosby, Malkin. The list goes on. Sometimes I don't think Pittsburgh is aware enough of what it's been able to witness on a nightly basis.

For me, the one thing that hasn't changed is the way I prepare for games. I do the same thing I've done for 45 years. Oh, I've added a few goal calls. That's for sure. My friend Joe Starkey asked me about the one I broke out in the Stanley Cup Final against San Jose.

"Oh, that makes you want to see a silly seal slide sideways in Sausalito!"

It just came into my brain in the middle of the night. I don't know why. It had nothing to do with San Jose. I mean, I had seen Sausalito and the seals when I was growing up in the Bay Area, but I don't know why it came to me. It was kind of like a dream.

Kind of like these past 50 years.

Mike Lange
October, 2016

TALES FROM THE
PITTSBURGH PENGUINS
LOCKER ROOM

THE EARLY YEARS

(1967–1974)

SKATING NUNS

The former Carol Dangerfield, wife of a team investor, gave Pittsburgh's NHL expansion club its nickname in 1967. For all the respect the name garnered, it might as well have come from Rodney Dangerfield.

The Pittsburgh *Penguins*?

Publicity director Joe Gordon was flabbergasted. He had to announce the name during a dinner at the swanky Pittsburgh Athletic Association.

People laughed.

"Can you imagine trying to promote a team whose nickname is the Penguins?" Gordon said later. "A penguin isn't the most graceful animal on the face of the earth. It waddles."

Head coach George "Red" Sullivan wasn't thrilled with the name, either.

"I can see it now," Sullivan told reporters. "The day after we play a bad game, the sportswriters will say, 'They skated like a bunch of nuns.'"

Officially, the team was named on February 10, 1967, after it fielded more than 26,000 entries from a newspaper contest. It even drew a winner, but the truth is that Carol McGregor, wife of investor John McGregor, came up with the name Penguins because she liked the alliteration, the possibility of black-and-white uniforms (it didn't happen) and the notion of penguins playing in the Igloo, the popular name for Pittsburgh's Civic Arena.

General manager Jack Riley was partial to the name Shamrocks, seeing as he and fellow Irishman Sullivan were running the show (and there had been a team called the Pittsburgh Shamrocks in the International Hockey League in the 1930s). Others favored Hornets, after Pittsburgh's championship minor-league team. Eskimos received consideration, too, but this team would be called the Penguins, a name quickly shortened to "Pens" in local vernacular.

A couple of decades later, the name took on new significance—and gained several measures of respect—when the Penguins were twice crowned league champions.

"I didn't think a hell of a lot of the name," Sullivan said later. "But it turned out to be OK."

DEATH OF A MASCOT

The Penguins' first mascot took the ice before games at the beginning of the 1968-69 season. There wasn't much glitter to his act.

"He just kind of waddled out and waddled off," goaltender Les Binkley said of Pete the Penguin, an Ecuadorian-born bird on loan from the Pittsburgh Zoo.

Average attendance that season was a franchise record-low 6,008, but Pete was well-loved—and much grieved when he died of pneumonia two months into the season.

Some of the players heard that Pete had been mishandled.

"He was a penguin, an animal, and they wanted to keep him warm," recalled defenseman Duane Rupp. "Well, he didn't want to be warm. He wanted to be cold."

"I remember that he died and that they brought in another one," Binkley said. "They called the second one 'Re-Pete.'"

LAST RITES

How tough was the Penguins' first coach, George "Red" Sullivan? Well, during his playing days, he was administered last rites after Montreal defenseman Doug Harvey speared him so hard he ruptured Sullivan's spleen.

In those days, teams would often play each other on back-to-back nights. Sullivan played for the Rangers, and on a Saturday in Montreal, he kicked the skates from under Harvey, who looked up and said, "I'll get you tomorrow, Sullivan."

The next night in New York, Harvey followed through on his threat. Sullivan went down. He got up and tried to play, but finally said, "I can't go." He was sent to a nearby hospital in a cab.

"I can remember the priest and the doctors standing around me," Sullivan said. "I was pretty sick."

He and Harvey never spoke about the incident. Harvey later played for Pittsburgh's Calder Cup–winning American Hockey League team, the Hornets.

TWO-MILLION-DOLLAR MAN

Joe Gordon, the Penguins' original publicity director, felt like a rich man when he accompanied team management to NHL headquarters in Montreal in June of 1967. That is where the Pittsburgh Penguins were announced as part of the NHL's six-team expansion. Gordon was carrying the team's $2 million entry fee in the form of a check.

"It was kind of exhilarating, even though it wasn't my money and there was nothing I could do with it," Gordon said. "To me, the most incredible thing looking back was that a franchise cost only $2 million."

CLEARING THE TRACK

Former Penguins general manager Jack Riley wasn't proud of the fact that he traded Rene Robert—a future member of Buffalo's famed "French Connection"—for aging winger Eddie Shack late in the 1971-72 season. But at least Pittsburgh got some serious entertainment value out of the deal.

There was nothing quite like a Shack-led rush. At 6-foot-1, 200 pounds, he was one of the league's bigger forwards, if not one of the more graceful ones.

"I used to tee it up for him and get out of there in a hurry," recalled goaltender Les Binkley. "He'd wind up and go behind the net, arms and legs and everything flailing."

Back in Toronto, when Shack played for the Maple Leafs, they used to say, "Clear the Track, here comes Eddie Shack!"

Legend has it that Shack couldn't read or write. When he played for the Maple Leafs, he'd heard that Detroit coach Jack Adams criticized him for not being able to spell. So when Shack scored against the Red Wings in the next game, he skated by the Detroit bench and said, "Hey, Jack: G-O-A-L.'"

In Pittsburgh, coach Leonard "Red" Kelly would write practice times on a blackboard.

"One time Red put on the blackboard, 'No practice tomorrow,'" Binkley said. "Eddie was the only guy who showed up."

On power plays, Shack would jump over the boards and say to his coach, 'OK, Leonard, who are the other four guys?'"

It wasn't as if Shack couldn't play. He had 25 goals in his only full season with the Penguins.

FASHION STATEMENT

It was believed that Jack Riley, the Penguins' first general manager, came up with the team's original colors of Colombia blue, Navy blue and white.

True?

"I'm guilty," Riley said.

Riley was from Toronto, where he followed the Argonauts of the Canadian Football League. They also used double shades of blue.

"Our light blue turned out too babyish blue," he said.

A local freelance artist named Bob Gessner designed the original logo featuring the skating penguin wearing a scarf in front of a gold triangle—symbolic of the city's Golden Triangle—but it was never used on a jersey, only on pucks and team letterhead. Publicity director Joe Gordon had the idea of putting a penguin on the Golden Triangle.

Sullivan, a former Rangers player, urged the team to use the diagonal "Pittsburgh" font, similar to the one the Rangers used. Ticket prices for home games at the Civic Arena in the Penguins' first season were $5, $4, $3.50 and $2.50—or about what various concessions would go for 30 years later.

THANKS, BUT NO THANKS

It seemed like an incredible opportunity for minor-league journeyman Jeannot Gilbert. A 26-year-old winger, he'd hooked on with the expansion Penguins in training camp of 1967 after several seasons with the Hershey Bears of the American Hockey League.

Two days before the season opener, just as he was about to sign a contract, Gilbert suddenly decided he wanted to go back to the

Clear the track! Eddie Shack moves in on Vancouver Canucks goalie Dunc Wilson. *(Photo courtesy of the Pittsburgh Penguins)*

minors. It didn't help that he'd taken a slash in the back of his legs during an exhibition game two nights earlier.

"I said, 'What's the matter, don't you want to play in the National Hockey League?'" GM Jack Riley remembered. "In his broken English, he said, 'No, I just like to play in Hershey.'"

Riley called Hershey boss Frank Mathers and asked if he wanted Gilbert back. Mathers said yes, because Gilbert was a talented scorer at that level. Riley asked who he could have in return.

Mathers shot back, "Who do you want?"

Riley wanted Gene Ubriaco, who scored 18 goals for the Penguins that season and years later became their coach.

MAGIC BUS

If it happened today, Bryan Watson figures, "I'd be in jail."

Luckily, it happened in the early 1970s, in Los Angeles, as the Penguins boarded a Marriott courtesy bus after traveling all day.

Somebody accidentally bumped the gear shift with an equipment bag, prompting Watson to jump behind the wheel to put the bus in park.

That would have been the end of it, but the bus driver—a "kid from the hotel"—reprimanded Watson, and anyone who knew the combative defenseman knew that wasn't a good idea.

This was a guy who body-checked his teammates in warmups, just to make sure they were ready.

"I got mad," Watson said. "And somebody in the back of the bus said, 'You don't have a hair on your [butt] unless you drive this thing to the hotel.'

"I said, 'If I can get this door closed, we're on our way, boys!' I was like Jackie Gleason in the *Honeymooners*.

"After I'd gone 50 feet, I realized, 'Holy Geez, I better be careful.' Everybody was going nuts, laughing, carrying on. You would have thought we were drunk, but that's the thing: We hadn't had a drink. Unfortunately, there were some regular people on the bus who were scared to death."

Once the team reached the hotel, coach Ken Schinkel called a meeting.

"He didn't want to know who did it," Watson said, "but he didn't want it to happen again, either."

CHAINSAW MASSACRE

Picking the Most Hated Penguin of all time is a near-impossible task. Darius Kasparaitis, Ulf Samuelsson, Gary Rissling, "Battleship" Bob Kelly, Rod Buskas, Dave Schultz, and many others would receive votes.

But if you asked opposing star forwards of the early 1970s, Bryan Watson might win by a landslide.

Watson, a defenseman acquired from Oakland in 1969, racked up 871 penalty minutes and at least that many resentments in only 303 games with the Penguins. Future Hall of Famers such as Gordie Howe and Bobby Hull positively despised Watson, who fed off the venom directed at him in opposing arenas.

Shortly after retiring, Watson nearly lost an arm in a chainsaw accident. Howe's reaction: "Oh yeah? How's the [freaking] chainsaw doing?"

This is the original Pittsburgh Penguins logo. *(Photo courtesy of the Pittsburgh Penguins)*

FIRST GAME

It seemed like a classic case of professional suicide when Penguins general manager Jack Riley petitioned the NHL to let his expansion team play its first game against the defending Stanley Cup-champion Montreal Canadiens.

It would mark the first time an expansion club played one of the NHL's established teams in the 12-team league, and it appeared to be a colossal mismatch.

There was a method to Riley's madness. "I figured if they could ever be taken, that was the time," he said.

It almost happened. The Canadiens escaped with a 2-1 victory on October 11, 1967, before a crowd of 9,307 (3,273 below capacity) at the Civic Arena.

"It was a hell of a hockey game," recalled Penguins coach George "Red" Sullivan.

Regal veteran Andy Bathgate, who wore a turtleneck under his jersey, scored for the Penguins, and the great Jean Beliveau scored the winner for Montreal, becoming just the third player in league history to reach the 400-goal plateau.

Afterward, legendary Montreal coach Toe Blake blasted his players.

"I never saw our team so nervous," he told reporters. "We must have given them the puck I don't know how many times. Stupid back-passes, something I've been harping on for two weeks. They proved they can still do it."

Rogie Vachon gained the victory for Montreal. He would get 33 more against the Penguins before his NHL career was finished, becoming the all-time winningest goaltender against them.

BOBBY CLARKE TO PENS?

The Penguins thought about drafting Bobby Clarke in 1969, but, like every other team, passed on the future Hall of Famer because they were concerned about his diabetes.

The Penguins instead took forgettable center Rick Kessell with the first pick of the second round (15th overall). The Philadelphia Flyers chose Clarke two picks later, after ignoring him in the first round.

How drastically would history have been altered if the Penguins had taken Clarke? Well, for one thing, they might not have gone 15

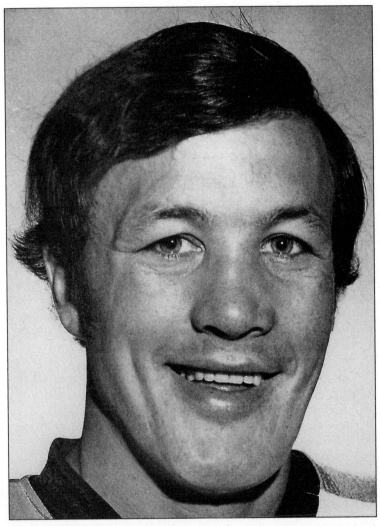

Bryan Watson took the hotel bus for a joy ride. *(Photo courtesy of the Pittsburgh Penguins)*

years and 42 games without a victory at the Spectrum in Philadelphia. The Flyers probably wouldn't have won two Stanley Cups, and the Penguins would have had two dynamic players from that draft. They took 5-foot-10, 160-pound center Michel Briere 26th overall.

Other teams ignored Briere because of his size. He had an outstanding rookie year in 1969-70 but died in an automobile accident that summer.

"We could have had both players," Riley said. "I've often wondered what that would have been like."

MICHEL BRIERE

Michel Briere knew how good he was, even if others had their doubts because of his smallish stature (5-foot-10, 160 pounds). The Penguins made him a third-round draft pick (26th overall) in 1969, the first year of the NHL Entry Draft, and he immediately asked for more money than they were offering.

General manager Jack Riley offered a $13,000 salary with a $4,000 signing bonus. Briere wanted a $5,000 bonus.

"I asked why," Riley recalled. "And he said, 'Because I'll be playing hockey in Pittsburgh for the next 20 years.'"

If only that pledge had come true. Two weeks after his marvelous rookie season—and three weeks before he was to be married—Briere sustained fatal injuries when his burnt-orange, 1970 Cougar failed to negotiate a curve on Highway 117 near his home in Malartic, Quebec. He was with two friends. It never was determined who was behind the wheel.

Ever the competitor, Briere held on for 11 months in a coma before he died on April 13, 1971, leaving behind a son, Martin.

"That was a big part of our franchise," Riley said.

Tragically, the ambulance that picked up Briere killed an 18-year-old bicyclist on the way to the hospital.

"It was one of Briere's friends," Riley said.

Riley and others visited Briere often as he lay in a hospital bed.

"I'd grab his hand and I'd say, 'Let's go, Mike, we've got to play St. Louis tonight'—that was our biggest rival—and he'd grab my hand tight," Riley said. "But as the visits went on, there was no communication at all."

Briere was third on the team in scoring that season, with 44 points (12 goals, 32 assists). He raised his game in the playoffs, leading the team in scoring with eight points. The Penguins finished just two victories short of the Stanley Cup final, losing to St. Louis in the semifinals.

"He was quite slight and small but very shifty and fast," recalled teammate Ron Schock. "He had a great attitude. I sat beside him in the dressing room. He was a real nice young kid. I liked him very much."

The number 21 already held esteemed status in Pittsburgh because it was worn by Pirates Hall of Fame outfielder Roberto Clemente, who, like Briere, died young.

About a week before the accident, Riley had spoken with Briere at a team function. Briere wanted a salary bump in year two, from $13,000 to $18,000.

"I knew he was worth it," Riley said. "I told him, 'We'll see in the fall.'"

• • •

Three weeks before his death, Michel Briere was to be married to Michele Beaudoin. The two already had a son, Martin, who was one year old at the time of the accident.

Thirty-five years later, a reporter found that Martin Briere was a successful Montreal architect with three sons—Arnaud, 7, Emile, 4, and Loic, 2—and a passion for the Penguins.

"I know my father's memory is still alive in Pittsburgh," Martin Briere told the *Pittsburgh Trib*. "I always follow the Penguins. It's something very important in our family.

"Everybody—my mother and my grandfather and myself—we all have a photo or a painting of my father wearing the Pittsburgh shirt. There are a lot of memories of that time. It's hard to not follow that hockey team."

WANT TO BUY A HOCKEY TEAM?

George Steinbrenner once had an interest in buying the Penguins. So did famous singer Andy Williams.

There were a whole bunch of other folks who actually went through with the idea . . . and were sorry they did. Nothing reflects the team's roller-coaster history more than the long line of men who've sunk money into what was a shaky proposition from day one.

Actually, before day one. A group of 21 owners invested $2 million to get the Penguins started in 1967. General manager Jack Riley remembered a request being made to hold the check a few extra days, just so more interest could be collected.

Michel Briere died tragically after an outstanding rookie season.
(Photo courtesy of the Pittsburgh Penguins)

Many of the same owners had invested in a soccer team called the Pittsburgh Phantoms, which played before miniscule crowds at Forbes Field and lost about $700,000 before the Penguins opened for business.

The Penguins' original publicity director, Joe Gordon, remembered that Peter Block, one of the Penguins' first investors, was convinced soccer represented the cutting edge of North American sports and would prove to be a money maker.

Gordon had his doubts about the Phantoms and the Penguins.

"You knew it was shaky because they had so many investors," he said. "You had a lot of guys who didn't have a lot of cash lying around."

Five months into the Penguins' first season, they were sold. Detroit banker Donald Parsons bought 80 percent of the team and started throwing money around. He promised each of his players in 1969-70 a $400 bonus if the team finished third or better in the Western Division. It did. He paid. But he soon was spent himself.

This would be a repeated theme among Penguins' owners.

"I really don't know all the ramifications," Riley said. "But I know this: When we went to the draft the first year Parsons was here, he picked me up in his private plane. The next year, we had to send him a plane ticket to Montreal, because the league was going to run the team."

The league did indeed run the team during the 1970-71 season, while Parson solicited offers. Before one game that season, Penguins defenseman Bryan Watson skated past NHL president Clarence Campbell and said, "Clarence, 'How's your team doing tonight?'"

BEER FOR BINK

Long before Eddie Johnston became a fixture in the Penguins organization, he was a popular goaltender for the Boston Bruins, and he treated his fellow goalies with the utmost respect.

Which is to say, he gave them beer.

After each game, the opposing goalie could find a six-pack in a bucket of ice with a towel over it, courtesy of "E.J."

That six-pack turned into a 12-pack for Penguins goalie Les Binkley on January 28, 1968, at the Boston Garden. In one of the more memorable performances in team history, Binkley made 33 saves in a 1-0 shutout, one of six he recorded that season. Most of his saves were of the spectacular variety against the most intimidating offensive machine in hockey.

The Penguins were dreadfully outplayed, but Binkley turned aside everything that Bobby Orr, Phil Esposito, Ken Hodge, Johnny Bucyk & Co. had to offer.

"It was one of those nights you couldn't do anything wrong," recalled Binkley, the Penguins' very first player.

Johnston didn't play that night—Gerry Cheevers tended goal for Boston—so he had a rink-side seat for Binkley's show.

"I don't think we flooded the ice in our end that night," Johnston said. "I sent a note that said, 'Bink, I know I usually send you six, but tonight I think you'll need a dozen.' We took care of each other."

Little-known defenseman George Konik scored the only goal in the game, thus becoming the answer to a trivia question. Konik is the answer to another trivia question, as well. He scored the first penalty-shot goal for the franchise, January 31, 1968, at St. Louis against legendary goaltender Glenn Hall.

SAVING FACE (OR NOT)

During the summers, Andy Brown loved to race dirt-track cars. During the season, he loved to face speeding pucks. And he did so without the benefit of a goalie mask.

In fact, on April 7, 1974, in a 6-3 loss to the Atlanta Flames, Brown became the last NHL goaltender to play a game without a shred of facial protection. This was a full 15 years after Toronto's Jacques Plante made history by becoming the first goalie to don a mask.

"Oh geez, Andy was a different guy, to say the least," recalled teammate Bryan Watson. "But he was a real competitor."

There were no limits on stick curves in those days, so shots often went wildly off target. Watson remembered seeing another goaltender, Gump Worsley, drop like a wounded elephant after absorbing a Bobby Hull slap shot to the ear.

"Hull shot it 100 mph," Watson said.

Plante first donned a mask on November 1, 1959, after a shot from New York Ranger—and future Penguin—Andy Bathgate cut him in the face.

The feisty Brown had 60 penalty minutes, fifth on the team, in 1973-74, which was his only full season. He signed with the WHAs Indianapolis Racers that summer. The historic game against the Flames proved to be the last of his NHL career.

MONEY ON THE FLOOR

In their third season (1969-70) the Penguins finished 12 games under .500 but made an unlikely run at the Stanley Cup, falling just two victories short of the final. They wouldn't get that close again for more than 20 years.

Their new coach was Hall of Famer Leonard "Red" Kelly, who'd learned a thing or two about motivating players during his playing career, when he was part of eight Cup-winning teams.

During the playoffs that year, Kelly borrowed a ploy he'd seen from legendary Toronto Maple Leafs coach Punch Imlach.

The Penguins had lost consecutive games to open a best-of-seven semifinal playoff series against the hated St. Louis Blues. Before Game 3, Kelly plunked anywhere from $1,300 to $7,250—depending on which story you believe—on the dressing-room floor.

This was back when playoff money could seriously pad a player's annual salary. In the Penguins' first season, for example, Andy Bath-

Andy Brown was the last NHL goalie to play a game without a mask.
(Photo courtesy of the Pittsburgh Penguins)

gate was the team's highest-paid player at $25,000. Most players took summertime jobs to increase their income.

Kelly looked at his troops and said, "This is what you're playing for. Don't let the other team reach their hand in it."

The players were awed.

"I never saw that many bills," goalie Les Binkley said. "I often wondered if anybody hung behind when we went on the ice that day. It's amazing how some coaches can get teams fired up."

The Penguins stormed back to win the next two games against Scotty Bowman's Blues but ultimately lost the series, four games to two.

SON OF A SEA COOK

Hockey players are renowned for using objectionable language, a fact that made the Penguins' second coach—and later general manager—Leonard "Red" Kelly, all the more remarkable. Kelly had been around the game his entire life, but he never was heard to swear during his three-plus seasons behind Pittsburgh's bench.

This, despite owning a .423 winning percentage.

When Kelly got really mad, he'd call somebody a "Son of a Sea Cook Bottle Washer" or exclaim, "Oh, what the hang's going on out there!'"

Suffice to say, nobody had a good answer to that question during the team's franchise-record, 18-game road winless streak in 1970-71.

And you wonder if Kelly might have sworn under his breath when he walked into his office one day to find Boston Bruins coach Harry Sinden watching Penguins game film. Apparently, a Penguins office worker had given Sinden the tapes and permission to watch them in Kelly's office.

"Red went nuts," recalled sportswriter Bill Heufelder, who covered the team for the *Pittsburgh Press*. "I don't think he swore, though."

HATIN' THE BLUES

Rivalries were an important part of the NHL landscape when the Penguins joined the league in 1967. Teams played each other 10 times a season, often in home-and-home series on the weekends.

The Penguins' first fierce rival was their Western Division partner, the St. Louis Blues, who inspired venomous hatred by trotting out the hell-bent-for-leather Plager brothers—Barclay, Bill, and Bob—plus defenseman Noel Picard and a host of others.

When a Pittsburgh sportscaster asked Penguins coach Leonard "Red" Kelly prior to a playoff series if there was bad blood between the teams, he replied, "Only if it spills."

The Blues weren't comprised only of troublemakers. There was a sense of royalty about them, as well. They had some magnificent offensive players and a pair of distinguished goaltenders in Glenn Hall and Jacques Plante. A young Scotty Bowman was the coach.

"When those guys all came down the runway in St. Louis, with the organ blasting, it was tremendous," recalled Bill Heufelder, who covered the Penguins for the *Pittsburgh Press*.

The Penguins countered with the likes of feisty goalie Al Smith, wacky defenseman Bryan Watson, and scrappy hustlers such as Bryan Hextall and Glen Sather.

NHL broadcaster Mike Emrick, then a freelance writer for a Pittsburgh suburban newspaper called the *Beaver County Times*, remembered covering an Easter Sunday game in 1970 at the Civic Arena. It ended with a controversial winning goal for the Penguins and with fans pelting the Blues with garbage.

After arena workers packed the litter into garbage cans, Barclay Plager dumped it back onto the ice.

"With Bobby and Barclay, what you saw is what you got," Watson said. "They were great competitors. They were showboats and the whole bit, but that was part of it. You knew it was going to be a slugfest."

Years later, Barclay Plager had former Penguins GM Jack Riley on his radio show and said to him, "Jack, you should've paid me to come to your building. Everyone hated me!"

MAYHEM

On January 23, 1974, a record crowd of 13,324 filled the Civic Arena expecting mayhem.

They weren't disappointed.

Six days earlier, new Penguins GM Jack Button acquired notorious tough guys "Battleship" Bob Kelly and Steve Durbano from the hated St. Louis Blues. This would be their first home game in a Penguins sweater.

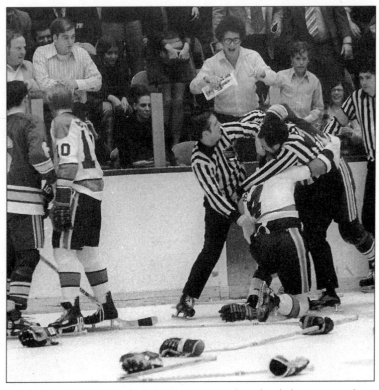

A common sight in the early days: The Penguins brawl with the St. Louis Blues. Notice the low glass. *(Photo courtesy of the Pittsburgh Penguins)*

"I remember we were standing at center ice during warm-ups, and Durby was talking to his old teammates," recalled former Penguins center Syl Apps. "He was saying, 'How are you? How are the kids? How's your son doing?' And the first time somebody comes in front of the net, he's spearing them, saying, 'You can't be standing here!'"

Early in the second period, Durbano fought Bob Gassoff while Kelly battled Barclay Plager. The crowd was delirious by the time the buzzer sounded in a 4-1 Penguins victory. Kelly and Durbano were named co-No. 1 stars of the game, a first in team history, and they skated onto the ice with their arms raised together. The photograph depicting that moment is among the more familiar and famous in team history.

"It's funny," Apps said. "After that, the teams that used to run around all over the place against us all of a sudden weren't running around anymore."

EAR MUFF MANIA

A by-product of the Penguins' rivalry with the St. Louis Blues was intense crowd participation. Penguins fans jeered Blues defenseman Barclay Plager by chanting his first name and held up signs like the one that said, "Bucket Mouth Bowman and His Three Stooges: Barclay, Bob and Noel."

That was in reference to Blues coach Scotty Bowman and three of his hellraisers: Barclay and Bob Plager and Noel Picard.

Blues fans weren't exactly wallflowers. "They used to go wild during the pregame stuff," recalled Penguins defenseman Duane Rupp.

In an effort to counteract that, and perhaps to send a message of sorts, Penguins coach Leonard "Red" Kelly made his players wear ear muffs at the start of a game January 3, 1970.

"He came in the dressing room and started passing out ear muffs, and the guys ware looking at each other like, 'Oh, man, we have to do this?'" Rupp said.

Rupp was spared the embarrassment, because he was in the starting lineup. Only players on the bench were forced to wear the ear muffs, which came in various colors.

Needless to say, it was a challenge to get through the National Anthem without laughing.

"We could barely stand on the blue line and keep a straight face," Rupp said.

The laughter died quickly. The Penguins lost, 6-0.

EMRICK ON THE SCENE

Most people know Mike Emrick as a national hockey broadcaster. Few know him as a freelance writer for a suburban Pittsburgh newspaper, but that's exactly what he was in the 1970 and '71, as he completed his studies at Geneva College in Beaver County, outside of Pittsburgh.

Emrick went to the editor of the *Beaver County Times* and said he'd cover Penguins home games for nothing if they got him a season pass.

Pittsburgh's Bob "Battleship" Kelly and Steve Durbano emerge as co-No. 1 stars after a game against St. Louis in which they roughed up their former teammates. *(Photo courtesy of the Pittsburgh Penguins)*

"I was a terrible writer," Emrick said. "But I was thrilled to be there."

THE CENTURY LINE

One was a Boston Bruins reject. Another had nearly retired because of multiple knee operations, and the third couldn't break a wet paper towel with his wrist shot.

Together, they were poetry on ice.

Jean Pronovost, Lowell MacDonald, and Syl Apps, all right-handed shots, comprised the first great line in Penguins history. Coach Ken Schinkel put them together in January of 1974. The three combined for 107 goals that season, second in the league to Buffalo's celebrated French Connection, and Penguins publicity director Terry Schiffhauer dubbed them "The Century Line."

The trio refused to play a dump-and-chase game, preferring more of a weaving, European style.

"We used to bump into each other more than anyone else would bump us," MacDonald said.

Technically, Apps was the center, MacDonald the left winger, and Pronovost the right winger, but the positions were interchangeable.

"Lowell and I couldn't shoot the puck any more than 15 feet; that's why we did a lot of passing," said Apps, the playmaker. "Plus, Lowell couldn't see that far. I think he had a worse shot than I did, but, boy, he could pick the spot. We were a little bit of a throwback in that we didn't dump the puck and we used a lot of drop passes."

MacDonald said teammates used to kid him, saying, "Geez, one of these times the puck will actually hit the back of the net."

His reply: "It just needs to get over that line, boys."

Apps came to the Penguins in January of '71 as part of an unpopular trade that sent gritty Glen Sather (later the architect of the Edmonton Oilers' dynasty) to the New York Rangers. The deal, orchestrated by Penguins coach and GM Leonard "Red" Kelly, proved to be among the best in team history.

The Pronovost deal wasn't bad either. GM Jack Riley acquired him from Boston in 1968 in exchange for a No. 1 draft pick that turned out to be nondescript winger Frank Spring. The gimpy-kneed MacDonald came along in the 1970 intra-league draft, when Kelly talked him out of retiring.

Apps said the three players rarely spent time together off the ice. Opponents wished they'd spent less time together on it.

POLISH ARMY

Franco's Italian Army goes down as the best-known ethnic rooting section in Pittsburgh sports history. It was founded by second- and third-generation Italian Americans who rooted for Steelers running back Franco Harris beginning in 1972.

Pittsburgh's Century Line, Lowell MacDonald, Jean Pronovost, and Syl Apps, celebrate Pronovost's 50th goal in 1976. *(Photo courtesy of the Pittsburgh Penguins)*

A few years before that, however, a group called Woytowich's Polish Army was in full bloom. Bob Woytowich was a rough-and-tumble Penguins defenseman who inspired a legion of followers.

As told in a *Pittsburgh Press* story from November 15, 1971, there were only two requirements for members of Woytowich's Polish Army: "You have to have the money to buy a general admission ticket, and you must never say a nice word about any of the Pens' opponents, collectively or individually."

PRESIDENTS DAY

Former Penguins goalie Les Binkley got knocked cold in a game one night. When the trainer came out to help him, he asked if Binkley could name the president of the United States.

"How should I know?" Binkley said. "I'm Canadian."

WILD WEEKEND

Going into the final weekend of the 1971-72 season, the Penguins couldn't have been all that optimistic about their playoff chances. They needed to tie or win at Philadelphia on Saturday, win at home against St. Louis on Sunday and hope the Buffalo Sabres won at Philadelphia.

Several minor miracles ensued.

The Penguins trailed 4-3 in the final minute at Philadelphia, but Greg Polis tied it with the goalie pulled at the 19:14 mark, tipping home Eddie Shack's low shot.

Before the next day's action, Penguins general manager Jack Riley called his colleague in Buffalo, Punch Imlach, with a word of encouragement. The irascible Imlach shot back, "You just take care of your game. We'll take care of ours."

As the Penguins were whipping the Blues, 6-2, the next night, the team made an announcement to the crowd that playoff tickets would go on sale if Buffalo was able to beat Philadelphia.

It didn't look good, because those teams went to the final minute tied 2-2. There still were eight minutes left in the Penguins' game when defenseman Dave Burrows went to the corner to retrieve a dump-in.

"As soon as I touched the puck, the building exploded with this huge cheer," Burrows said. "I thought there was a fight somewhere. I don't know if I left the puck there or turned around to look for a fight. It almost cost us, because guys were coming down on me."

Fans roared because the out-of-town scoreboard showed that Buffalo had won. The Sabres pulled it out on Gerry Meehan's desperation, 45-foot shot that sailed through the pads of Flyers goalie Doug Favell with only four seconds left (there was no overtime in those days).

"Suddenly, there was this stampede to the box office," Riley said.

Eighteen years later, the Penguins again would go to the final day of the regular season with Buffalo intimately involved in their playoff hopes. That time, however, Uwe Krupp's long slap shot in overtime at the Civic Arena gave Buffalo a 3-2 victory and sent the Penguins home for the summer.

The good news is that the Penguins got to draft fifth overall and used the selection on future superstar Jaromir Jagr.

THE IGLOO

Pittsburgh's hockey arena was compared to a giant silver spaceship. Originally built to house the Civic Light Opera, it was completed in 1961 at the cost of $22 million and has the largest retractable dome roof in the world (although it was never opened during a hockey game).

That's 170,000 square feet and 2,950 tons of pure Pittsburgh steel.

The other unique part of the Penguins' home rink, when the team broke into the league, was the sheet of ice. It was bigger than in most arenas. The standard NHL rink nowadays measures 200 feet long by 85 feet wide. Former Penguins winger Lowell MacDonald said the Civic Arena's sheet measured 207 x 92 until it was revamped in the mid-1970s to make way for some expensive seats.

MacDonald and his linemates, Syl Apps and Jean Pronovost, played a passing game that lent itself nicely to the big rink.

"Prony had a great set of wheels, I could skate, and Syl had a great sense of where we were and what we were doing," MacDonald said. "It was a great rink to play in when it was a bigger ice surface. We had at least one or two years there, as a line, before they took it away from us."

The fans inside the dome were pretty unique, too. Defenseman Dave Burrows grew up in Toronto, where the fans have always been knowledgeable and polite. Penguins fans were neither when the team came into existence.

"When I got there [in 1971], the fans were wild," said Burrows, whose workmanlike efforts eventually landed him in the team's Hall of Fame. "There were a lot of blue-collar workers, and they loved the physical part of it and would be so vocal about the game.

"I mean, in Toronto, people would cheer and stuff, but in Pittsburgh, people would fight in the stands. We loved it. When we started winning there for a while, I remember we had a string of sellouts, and I was just dying to get on the ice. I loved Pittsburgh and loved the people. They seemed to appreciate the style of hockey I played, I guess. They were very good for me."

SURVEY SAYS

One thing about the late Al Smith: "You never had any idea what he was going to do," said teammate Ron Schock.

Smith was the anti-establishment goalie during his two seasons with the Penguins. A real rebel.

"You could put him in a $3,000 suit, and he'd still look like he came out of an alleyway," Schock said.

On one particular road trip, Smith decided to conduct a survey on the best ways to attract women. He carried around a notebook, madly scribbling answers to questions like, "What kind of shaving cream do you use?" and "What's your opening line?" He interviewed players, stewardesses, anyone he could find.

"He did this the whole road trip," Schock recalled.

Smith's preliminary data showed that common strategies did not work and that people who wore unusual cologne or delivered weird opening lines experienced the most success.

Before he could issue a final report, however, straight-laced coach Leonard "Red" Kelly intervened. Schock remembers Kelly approaching Smith in front of the team and saying, "Smitty, that's enough with the survey. . . . You'll never get a woman, anyways."

Smith went home and burned the survey in his bathtub.

Pittsburgh's (Civic) Mellon Arena. *(Photo courtesy of the Pittsburgh Penguins)*

FRENCH CONNECTION

The Buffalo Sabres had the most famous French Connection, but it was together only for part of the 1970s. The Penguins' French Connection has spanned nearly the entire history of the franchise.

It's easy to connect the dots. Start with a stately winger named Jean Pronovost, who hailed from Shawinigan Falls, Quebec. He became the first Penguin to score 30 goals, in 1971-72, and the first to score 50, in 1975-76.

"He was an underrated, dedicated player who rarely had an off game," recalled former linemate Syl Apps.

During Pronovost's rookie year, a small-framed centerman named Michel Briere was racking up 161 points in 50 games for the Shawinigan Bruins of the Quebec Major Junior Hockey League. That summer, the Penguins drafted 5-foot-10, 160-pound Briere 26th overall and watched him blossom into an impact player in his rookie year. His life tragically was cut short by a car accident shortly after that season.

Briere had also played a bit of junior hockey for the Sorel Blackhawks of the QMJHL. Five years later, a flashy young Sorel forward named Pierre Larouche set a Canadian junior hockey record by logging 251 points in 67 games. Larouche's brother, Maurice, had played junior with Briere.

The Penguins took Pierre Larouche eighth overall. He scored 31 goals as a rookie and 50 in his second year, becoming, at 20, the youngest NHL player ever to score 50 goals.

In 1977, Larouche was traded to Montreal, the birthplace of a kid named Mario Lemieux, who in 1983-84 smashed Larouche's single-season junior points record (although Larouche's record of 157 assists stayed intact). Lemieux piled up 282 points in 70 games with Laval of the QMJHL. He would become one of the greatest players in NHL history and would be the team owner when the Penguins drafted yet another ballyhooed QMJHL product, goaltender Marc-Andre Fleury, first overall in 2003.

Fleury made the Penguins roster as an 18-year-old and stopped 46 of 48 shots in his NHL debut. For a short time at the start of his career, he lived with Lemieux's family.

Oh, and Fleury was born in Sorel, where Briere and Larouche played junior hockey.

GONE FISHIN'

It might just be an old fish story, but former Penguins equipment manager John Doolan swears it's true.

The team returned to the Civic Arena at about 3 a.m. after a bus trip to Buffalo—no word on whether alcohol was served—when to their delight they discovered an outdoorsman show set up for the next day. It included a pool of trout, where kids could fish for prizes.

Players such as goalie Les Binkley and center Bryan Hextall suddenly rediscovered their inner children.

"The guys saw all these trout, grabbed a big net from one of the booths and started scooping," Doolan said. "One guy went right in the pool, about two feet deep.

"People from the show came in the next day and wondered where all the trout were."

2

ON THE BRINK

(1975–1983)

JOHN DENVER'S FAULT?

No team, not even the Philadelphia Flyers, has tortured the Penguins more than the New York Islanders, who administered three devastating playoff blows between 1975 and 1993.

One nearly proved fatal to Pittsburgh's eight-year-old NHL franchise.

It occurred in the spring of 1975, as the Penguins became the second team in league history to blow a three-games-to-none lead in a best-of-seven series.

Many of the players who participated cite a delay between Games 3 and 4 at Nassau Coliseum as the turning point.

Game 4 should have been played on a one-day rest, but a John Denver concert fouled things up. The game was moved to two days after the concert—to Sunday, April 20—so it could be televised nationally.

Somewhere in there, the Penguins lost their edge. Or so some say.

"I never quite forgave John Denver," said former Penguins captain Ron Schock. "I think the momentum turned with that concert."

Teammate Syl Apps wished the Penguins had flown back to Pittsburgh between Games 3 and 4. But the team was hemorrhaging money.

"Back then, you'd say, 'What's it going to cost us to go home?'" Apps said. "Today, they would have flown out right after that third game."

One former Penguin, Pierre Larouche, strongly disagrees with the notion that the delay caused a shift in momentum. He said it simply was a matter of overconfidence.

"After the third game, management threw a party for us," recalled Larouche, then a rookie. "And everybody thought it was over. It was not. You can't use the delay as an excuse. We got whacked."

CARD SHARK

One night, former Penguins general manager Baz Bastien took out his glass right eye and put it on the table during a card game. Another player looked at him and said, "Baz, quit looking at the cards."

TRASH MAN

Hockey players are a superstitious sort, sometimes to the point of psychosis. Take goaltender Nick Ricci, for example. He couldn't walk past a trash can before going onto the ice.

His reasoning?

"If you walk by trash, you'll play like garbage."

When Ricci first was recalled from the minors in 1979, he asked equipment man John Doolan to move all the trash cans.

After a while, however, it became clear that all the superstition in the world wasn't going to help Ricci.

"He wasn't doing anything," Doolan recalled, "so I finally said, 'Hey, enough of this,' and moved the trash cans back to where they were."

SHEDDEN'S GRANDMOTHER

There wasn't much to laugh about during the Penguins' 8-2 loss at Toronto on January 24, 1983.

Well, not until Doug Shedden's grandmother made her way to the team bench.

Shedden had grown up near Toronto, so several family members were in attendance, including his grandmother. There was an exit at Maple Leaf Gardens where fans could walk right past the visiting team's bench, and, sure enough, an elderly woman came down to comfort her grandson . . . with about eight minutes left in the game . . . and the puck in play.

"She gave me a big hug and kiss and said, 'Don't you worry about it, there'll be better days,'" Shedden remembered. "I said, 'Nanny, Nanny, it's OK. Go back and sit in your seat.'"

Coach Eddie Johnston was dumbfounded. Shedden's teammates were folded over in laughter.

"There were about nine guys who had to put their heads under the boards," he said, "because their faces were turning purple."

MISTAKEN IDENTITY?

Legend has it that then-general manager Baz Bastien, on October 18, 1978, sent a first-round draft pick to the Montreal Canadiens believing that the player he acquired—Rod Schutt—actually was future Hall of Famer Steve Shutt.

Rod Schutt insists it's a fable.

"That was actually a locker-room joke," Schutt said. "Guys would say, '[Bastien] only has one eye, so he only saw the last name.' It wasn't true, because he knew quite well who he was getting. Pittsburgh was going to draft me originally, and we had conversations before the draft."

Schutt laughed and added, "Every once in a while he used to call me Steve."

HIS TEETH FELL OUT

The poor girl who told Jimmy Roberts his room at the Forum Inn wasn't ready probably still remembers his reaction.

As broadcaster Mike Lange remembers it, Roberts, an assistant coach for the Penguins in the mid-1980s, was tired and cranky after a full day of travel. A lot of the guys were, because the team had just traversed the country. They were playing the Los Angeles Kings the next night at the Great Western Forum.

When the young hotel desk worker told Roberts none of the rooms was ready—that, in fact, there were no reservations for the Pittsburgh Penguins—he lost it.

"You have to know Jimmy," Lange said. "He was part of the old guard, played for the Canadiens in the '70s and believed in playing hard and working hard at your job.

"He said, 'This is the *Pittsburgh Penguins*, we're staying here, 25 rooms, we're spending a lot of money here.' She said, 'I don't have the keys, I don't have the rooms, but if you can wait, we'll clean the rooms.'

"Jimmy slams his hand on the counter again, and when he hit it, his bridge came out of his mouth, flew in the air and came down on the counter. This girl was 20 at most. Her eyes got big as a frisbee. Well, in the same motion, Jimmy picked up his teeth with his left hand—didn't miss a beat—and kept yelling."

Word traveled quickly. A brutal day suddenly became bearable.

"One of the funniest moments I've experienced," Lange said.

SPINNER SPENCER

Brian "Spinner" Spencer played only 86 games for the Penguins, from 1977 to 1979, but no one who shared the smallest part of that time with him will ever forget.

"He was unique," recalled teammate Greg Malone, whose family housed Spencer for a time. "If you got to know him, he'd give you the shirt off his back."

Former Penguins winger Lowell MacDonald remembered a vintage Spinner moment from a slow afternoon in Los Angeles, when the Penguins arrived early for practice.

Three players decided to wage a contest to see who could chew the most pieces of gum. One finally gagged and spit his wad into a garbage can. The curly-haired Spencer, who'd been watching silently, walked to the trash can, fished it out and stuffed it in his mouth.

He added a few fresh pieces and won the contest.

"That was Spinner at his best," MacDonald said. "He sat there watching this thing, and then he figured out a way to win with a whole lot less effort. He had a lot of guys rolling on the floor."

The bad times, however, far outweighed the good in Spencer's life. Both he and his father were shot to death in separate incidents, 18 years apart.

His father, Roy Spencer, was killed in a shootout with Royal Canadian Mounted police after holding a Canadian Broadcasting Company television station in Prince George, British Columbia, at gunpoint. He was incensed because the station did not carry his son's NHL debut with the Toronto Maple Leafs that night after it had announced it would.

Eighteen years later, Brian Spencer was shot to death in a friend's pick-up truck in Florida. He had reportedly been involved with several shady characters.

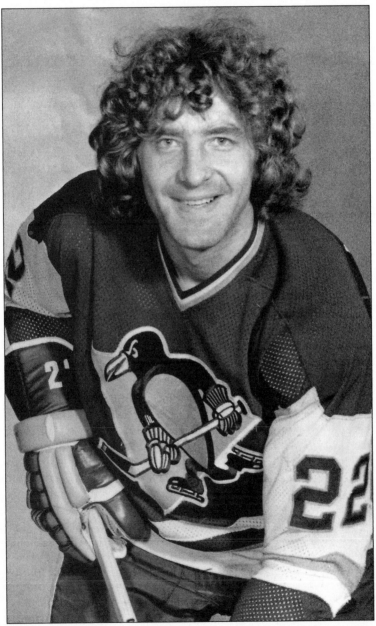

Brian "Spinner" Spencer made the dressing room a lively place.
(Photo courtesy of the Pittsburgh Penguins)

Those who knew Spencer well said he had a big heart and lots of quirks.

"He could draw pictures like you wouldn't believe," Malone said. "He was also chiseled, with big, strong fingers and toes. He used to jump on a table and land on it with his toes curled, then jump back down and land on his toes."

NOT SO SILENT NIGHT

A 5-3 loss at Minnesota on December 23, 1978, could not dampen the Penguins' spirits. The team was winning regularly, and it was headed home for the holidays.

Maybe that explains why hulking forward Peter Mahovlich was compelled to orchestrate a round of Christmas carols.

"There he was, with sheet music, leading the carols," recalled goaltender Greg Millen. "I'll never forget it as long as I live—a six-foot-five guy on a Continental Airlines commercial flight singing away. It was incredible. Everybody sang."

'WE HAVE A PROBLEM'

Former Penguins trainer Kenny Carson figured it would be a nice gesture to lend the Penguins' equipment truck to winger Lowell MacDonald in the summer of 1975, as long as MacDonald brought it back before training camp.

MacDonald had a lot of things to move from Pittsburgh to his new summer home in Nova Scotia, so he accepted Carson's offer and drove his family in the large truck adorned with Penguins logos.

A month later, MacDonald got a phone call. It was Carson.

"He says, 'We have a problem. The team has gone bankrupt, and they tell me we need to have all the assets here,'" MacDonald said. "I said, 'Kenny, I am not driving the truck 1,280 miles back to Pittsburgh. You have to be kidding. If they want it bad enough, they can either come get it or call the Mounties.'"

NEW LOWS

The 1983-84 Penguins generally are regarded as the worst team in franchise history. A team-record 48 players were used, and the club finished with a franchise-worst 38 points.

The season-ticket base was 2,170 in the 16,033-seat arena, and the team lost $5 million. People were sure the Penguins were going to move. Some of the fans who bothered to show up did so with bags on their heads.

"You had so few fans that the boo birds would really stick out," remembered winger Bob Errey, then a rookie. "I remember coming down the runway and hearing the chants—'Errey sucks!'—or something like that. I couldn't give away tickets back then. The one promising thing was that if we did get last place, we'd be able to pick up this French-Canadian kid named Mario Lemieux."

ONE-MAN CLUB

When Eddie Johnston joined the Penguins organization as coach in 1980, the team did not have a farm club. It wouldn't own one until 1999, but at least it had affiliations. Johnston didn't even have that his first year.

"We had 23 guys, total, at training camp," he said. "And [left winger] Jim Hamilton was our farm club."

LOUD AND CLEAR

Late Penguins general manager Baz Bastien was known to fly off the handle now and again, which is why defenseman Ron Stackhouse made it a point to stuff cotton balls in his ears whenever Bastien addressed the team.

Stackhouse would nod his head in the affirmative, as if he were listening, then remove the cotton when Bastien left.

Rookie centerman Mark Johnson probably wished he had some cotton after what Bastien said to him in 1981, following the Penguins' decisive, double-overtime playoff loss to the St. Louis Blues.

Johnson had missed a golden chance in each overtime, hitting three posts on two chances. "Kid, you coulda' been a hero tonight," Bastien said, "but you blew it."

HISTORY ALTERED

Nobody knows for sure exactly what turned the Penguins' playoff series against the New York Islanders in 1975. All that's certain is that the Penguins squandered a three-games-to-none lead—and that both franchises never were the same.

The Penguins sank into bankruptcy that summer. The Islanders moved toward a dynasty that would result in four consecutive Stanley Cups (1980-83).

"I always wondered if we'd won—and we're talking winning one more game—what would we have gone on to?" former Penguins defenseman Dave Burrows said. "You look at the Islanders, they went on to become a dynasty. That gave them the confidence to be a Stanley Cup team."

"We made the Islanders," added former Penguins winger Lowell MacDonald. "Their attendance was not good, but once they turned it around, they picked it up and were never the same after that. I still believe their guys should have sent us thank-you cards. That franchise was in bad shape. We weren't anywhere near the condition they were in."

That's debatable, considering the Penguins were $6.5 million in debt and soon to be bankrupt. If they'd won that series, they would have earned enough revenues in the next round to avert bankruptcy.

Then again, if they'd won that series, they might not have sunk to the point they did in the early 1980s—and Mario Lemieux might never have worn a Penguins sweater.

Along that line of thinking, the 1975 Penguins actually did the franchise a favor.

Right?

"Damn right we did," Syl Apps said.

STAN GILBERTSON

Sometimes, there is humor in tragedy. Such a time occurred at Penguins training camp in 1978, when left winger Stan Gilbertson stood on a scale at the Civic Arena, not long after losing his leg in a jeep accident.

Head coach Johnny Wilson had been pestering Gilbertson about his weight before the accident. When Gilbertson was released from the hospital, he went to the arena, stepped on a scale and started yelling, "Johnny! Johnny!"

Wilson thought Gilbertson had fallen or dropped his crutches. When he ran into the room, Gilbertson looked at him and said, "I made weight, Johnny, I made weight!"

TAKE THIS JOB . . .

Talk about ending a career in style. Lou Morrison, a nondescript right winger who played for the Penguins from 1974-78, decided he'd had enough as he and a few teammates drove to his summer home on the Jersey shore.

Morrison stopped his car at the top of a bridge, opened the trunk and threw his equipment bag into the ocean.

"He said, 'I'll never play another hockey game,'" equipment manager John Doolan recalled. "At an alumni game the next year, he said he needed equipment, and I said, 'Oh yeah? Get a fishing line.'"

One of Morrison's former teammates, defenseman Tom Edur, retired at age 23 and became a Jehovah's Witness.

NEVER AGAIN

Ed Johnston was the most recent goalie to play every minute of every game in a single season.

A torn ear lobe, three broken noses, and 70 stitches failed to keep Johnston from missing a second of the 1963-64 season with the Boston Bruins.

"That's something that will stand forever," said former Penguins goaltender Ron Tugnutt.

Remembered Johnston: "The trainer was the back-up goalie. That was for all teams. You only had one goalie then."

Johnston, who played without a mask, finished the season with a record of 18-40-12—that's 70 games—with a 3.01 goals-against average. The closest he came to missing any action was when a slap shot tore his left earlobe. He got it stitched and returned to the crease.

He wasn't so lucky at other times in his career. When he got hurt badly enough to leave a game, a back-up goalie—if it wasn't the trainer—had to be pulled from the crowd. One time it was a fireman.

"It was a fire chief in Boston, and I had to hold his leg down it was shaking so bad," Johnston said. "He was nervous."

BROKEN GLASS

All the losing in the mid-1980s was enough to make a guy want to eat glass.

Literally.

Paul Steigerwald, the Penguins' radio play-by-play man, remembers going on TV in 1984 and saying that defenseman Bryan Maxwell was struggling because of a knee injury.

This did not please Maxwell, who took great exception to the term "struggling." He confronted Steigerwald, who recounted their brief but memorable interaction.

"He took a wine glass, bit it, chewed it up into a million pieces and spit into the palm of my hand."

BANKRUPT

The Penguins are the only franchise in National Hockey League history that could answer, "Which time?," if somebody asked when they had gone bankrupt.

The first time occurred in 1975, although technically the franchise did not declare bankruptcy but was placed in "receivership" with a debt of $6.5 million.

No one who worked at the Civic Arena will forget the sight of Penguins employees scrambling to recover their belongings before the IRS padlocked the doors to the Penguins' offices.

The IRS had slapped the Penguins with a $532,000 lien for failure to pay withholding taxes.

"They came in and took files and everything else," said Elaine Heufelder, who worked at the arena and would later work for the Penguins. "It was a mad scramble. It was funny but not funny, if you know what I mean."

Yes, the players knew exactly what that meant. That season had been a constant exercise in cutting corners.

"There were things that went on, with nickeling and diming everyone," defenseman Dave Burrows recalled. "You only got one towel in the dressing room, and we used to have oranges in the dressing room, and then they cut those out, and you'd think, 'Geez, we're in awful shape.'

"We were all worried. As a player, you don't want to go through a summer thinking, 'What are you going to do with your house?'"

Pens coach Eddie Johnston gives an earful to a linesman. *(Photo courtesy of the Pittsburgh Penguins)*

"Conditions were not ideal," added former centerman Syl Apps. "If you had a dozen sticks, you'd be lucky. I remember a couple times, guys only had one pair of skates. If you broke a blade, too bad."

A year later, the Penguins hired a general manager who was used to working in such conditions. They brought in Baz Bastien, who'd been the assistant general manager for the bankrupt Kansas City Scouts.

BENCH-CLEARING BRAWL

The night before the Pittsburgh Steelers played in their last Super Bowl under coach Chuck Noll, the Penguins went bonkers at the Civic Arena, setting a franchise penalty-minute record with a lot of help from the Edmonton Oilers.

The trouble began when defenseman Kim Clackson drilled 18-year-old Oilers phenom Wayne Gretzky after Gretzky missed a scoring chance. Oilers tough guy Dave Semenko took great exception.

Order wasn't restored for more than an hour.

The Oilers were the first to leave their bench, a fact that prompted Penguins captain Orest Kindrachuk to wave to his bench for reinforcements. Clackson and Semenko fought three times, including once with Clackson in the penalty box.

Oilers coach Glen Sather threw a water bottle and reportedly tried to climb the glass to get at a heckler.

"Clackson deliberately tried to injure Gretzky with his stick," Sather told reporters after the game. "A goof like that shouldn't be in the league. That stuff went out with the dark ages."

Each team had four players ejected, and the game took nearly three hours. The last fight of the night saw the Oilers' Colin Campbell—the NHL's future Lord of Discipline—square off with Greg Malone with 2:45 remaining.

The Penguins were assessed 144 penalty minutes. The teams combined for 247. Penguins defenseman Russ Anderson set a team mark with 51 penalty minutes himself.

The next day, Anderson and his wife modeled the team's new black-and-gold jerseys at a team function on scenic Mt. Washington. And the Steelers beat the Los Angeles Rams, 31-19.

FOUR-GOAL NIGHT

For a 15-year stretch beginning in 1974, trips to Philadelphia were like trips to the dentist for the Penguins. It wasn't always a treat when the Flyers visited the Civic Arena, either.

On one such visit—December 13, 1980—Paul Gardner became the first player in Penguins history to score four goals in a game. To no avail. Flyers star Bobby Clarke countered with a hat trick in a 6-5 victory.

Still, it was a night to remember for Gardner, who excitedly ambled up to the wives' room shortly after the final buzzer.

"Even the wives gave me a standing ovation," he said.

Gardner was the ultimate garbage man in front of the net.

"We used to joke that you had to get it by him and the goaltender to score a goal," teammate Randy Carlyle said.

LUCKY PIERRE

During the 1975-76 season, at age 20, Penguins forward Pierre Larouche became the youngest player in NHL history to score 50 goals.

"Lucky" Pierre, as he was called, also became one of the only players, presumably, to be put in a kissing booth at a shopping mall. It happened in the summer of 1976, when he and teammate Wayne Bianchin were asked to staff the booth for charity.

Each kiss was worth $1 to Children's Hospital.

"Oh my God, I felt like Elvis Presley that day," Larouche remembered. "I went to the mall with all those cops around me and all those people. It was pretty wild. I didn't want to go."

Well, it wasn't a bad thing once the kissing started, was it?

"All depends," Larouche said. "And if my mom would've seen me, she would've died."

Around the same time, popular Pittsburgh sportscaster Myron Cope hosted a contest called "Win A Date With Pierre." More than 15,000 letters poured in, each woman stating in 20 words why she would like to go out with Larouche.

One letter stood out.

"It was a Philly girl, the niece of [Flyers goalie] Bernie Parent, and she said if she didn't win, she'd have the Broad Street Bullies kick the hell out of me," Larouche said. "I saw it and said, 'You don't have to worry about that; they're already doing it.'"

LOOK MA, NO HAIR

Paul Gardner had just been acquired from the Toronto Maple Leafs in November of 1980. He was nervous as he walked late into the Penguins dressing room to meet his new teammates. One of them was left winger Ross Lonsberry.

What Gardner saw next nearly made him run for his life.

"[Lonsberry] sat down and took off his toupee," Gardner said. "It caught me by surprise because I'd played against him and never knew."

Lonsberry kept the toupee on the top shelf of his locker stall. One time, at gate 3 at the old Chicago Stadium, he pushed the door open on a typically windy winter's night, and the toupee blew off his head.

"He had to run and chase it down," broadcaster Mike Lange said.

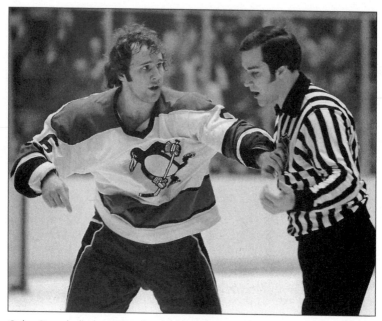

Colin Campbell, the NHL's future czar of discipline, was a scrapper with the Penguins. *(Photo courtesy of the Pittsburgh Penguins)*

Lonsberry removed the toupee for games and practices, leaving nothing but a bald head under his helmet. Gardner doubts Lonsberry would admit it, but he wore a buckle on his helmet, while everyone else used a clip.

STRANGE COMPANY

Guess who Islanders forward Eddie Westfall drank with the night he eliminated the Penguins from the 1975 playoffs?

The Penguins, that's who.

Westfall could barely think straight after scoring the only goal in Game 7 of an exhilarating but exhausting series that saw the Islanders erase a three-games-to-none deficit and win the final game in Pittsburgh.

"I just remember sitting there, reflecting on the series," Westfall said. "By the time I looked up, everybody was gone except the trainers. When I got dressed and went outside the locker room, I couldn't find any of my teammates."

Westfall encountered center Syl Apps and some other Penguins in an arena corridor. Apps wondered why Westfall was all by himself.

"I told him, 'Everybody left. Where are you guys going?'" Westfall said. "He said, 'The Pleasure Bar.' So I went with the Penguins players and their wives to the Pleasure Bar and sat there drinking until sunrise."

Westfall and Apps had plenty to talk about: Apps' father, Syl Sr., played for Toronto in 1942, when the Maple Leafs became the first team in NHL history to rally from a three-games-to-none deficit to win a playoff series.

BLACK AND GOLD

Much to the chagrin of the Boston Bruins, the Penguins wore black and gold uniforms for the first time on January 30, 1980, in a 4-3 loss to the St. Louis Blues.

The Penguins were looking to capitalize on Pittsburgh's new "City of Champions" status and attract more fan support by switching from their familiar blue and white. The Super-Bowl champion Pittsburgh Steelers and the World Series-champion Pittsburgh Pirates both wore black and gold.

So did the Bruins, who lodged a protest with the league. The Penguins prevailed by arguing that a black and gold precedent had been set by the Pittsburgh Pirates NHL hockey club in the early 1920s.

TRAGEDY STRIKES

On March 15, 1983, Penguins general manager Baz Bastien died in a car accident on his way home from a dinner sponsored by the Professional Hockey Writers Association.

The Associated Press account of the accident went like this:

"Penguins general manager Allege 'Baz' Bastien, his driving impaired by alcohol and the loss of one eye, died after his car rammed a motorcycle, authorities say."

Earlier in the evening, marketing director Paul Steigerwald spent time with Bastien, a colorful, cigar-chomping, old-time hockey guy who often paced the Civic Arena halls at break-neck speed.

"It was about 5 p.m., and he was puffing on a cigar and sipping on a cocktail he had poured from a bottle he kept in a cabinet behind his desk," Steigerwald said. "Baz was in a reflective mood that day, so I started asking him questions about the loss of his eye (during a practice when he played goalie decades earlier), his previous heart bypass surgery and other personal matters."

Bastien, one of the true characters of the game, had been the coach of the Pittsburgh Hornets' Calder-Cup winning AHL team in 1967. He went on to have the second longest tenure (527 games) of any Penguins GM except Craig Patrick but had a winning percentage of just .447.

One of the highlights of Bastien's career came on June 13, 1978, when he acquired defenseman Randy Carlyle and winger George Ferguson in exchange for defenseman Dave Burrows.

Ferguson won a playoff series against Buffalo with an overtime goal in 1979, and Carlyle won the Norris Trophy as the league's best defenseman two years later.

THE INCREDIBLE HULK

The late Brian "Spinner" Spencer earned his nickname for his whirling-dervish style of play. Off the ice, he put his manic energy into building a mind-boggling vehicle he called, "The Incredible Hulk."

It was a $35,000, diesel-powered vehicle that took four years to build. It had the body of a Dodge van sitting atop a 2.5-ton US Army surplus truck skeleton.

And that wasn't all.

"His whole dash was covered with all kinds of instruments he took from an airplane," recalled teammate Greg Malone. "If he went over a pothole, he could tell you how deep it was and all this stuff because of the instruments he had."

The Penguins released Spencer in 1979, a day after he said to eminent broadcaster Bob Prince during a televised interview, "I don't want to be associated with a bird that can't fly."

SUPERSTAR

Pierre Larouche was the first flamboyant star in Penguins history. The buzz began when GM Jack Button drafted Larouche eighth overall in 1974.

Larouche had scored 94 goals and a league-record 251 points the year before in the Quebec Major Junior Hockey League. He notched a hat trick in his first training camp scrimmage and wound up with 33 goals in his rookie season.

He also rankled a few teammates with his cocky demeanor.

"We all came from the old school, and he was kind of in the new generation," winger Lowell MacDonald said. "But he came in with unbelievable hype, and he lived up to it."

Equipment man John Doolan saw as much when he rejoined the Penguins in 1976.

"Before my first game back, Pierre skated by me and said, 'Kid, I'll show you what they pay me to do here,'" Doolan said.

On the second-period faceoff, Larouche raked the puck from Philadelphia's Bobby Clarke, skated through the Flyers and deked goalie Bernie Parent for a spectacular goal.

NO ICE?

When the Penguins showed up in Johnstown, Pennsylvania, for training camp in 1982, they were greeted with a slight problem.

No ice.

A combination of warm weather and machine malfunction at the Johnstown War Memorial Arena—site of filming for the movie *Slapshot*—put camp plans on hold.

"Half the guys headed back to Pittsburgh, and half the guys headed to the golf course," recalled center Greg Malone. "Practices were canceled for two days."

Said winger Paul Gardner: "It was pretty comical. It was also beautiful outside, so we just kind of walked the streets for a few days. That was different."

ONE GOAL: MARIO

Eddie Johnston will deny the accusation, but it seemed rather obvious that he, shall we say, "created conditions by which his team found it difficult to win."

Johnston, then the Penguins' general manager, knew that by finishing last overall, the Penguins would be guaranteed a chance to take Mario Lemieux, the sort of player, Johnston said, who "comes along once in a lifetime. Maybe."

It's not as if Johnston had to work overtime to make sure his '83-84 team stunk. It wasn't exactly rife with overachievers. But he helped push it over the edge by doing things like sending goaltender

Roberto Romano to the minors late in the season when Romano was playing well.

In his place, Johnston brought up a goalie by the name of Vincent Tremblay, who allowed 24 goals in four games . . . his only games in a Penguins sweater and last of his NHL career.

In early March, Johnston traded defenseman Randy Carlyle, three years removed from winning the Norris Trophy as the league's best defenseman, to the Winnipeg Jets for a player to be named later.

Much later. Moe Mantha arrived after the season.

Carlyle had been injured, but on the morning of the trade, he told Penguins management he was ready to play that night.

Meanwhile, players were constantly shuffled back and forth from the minors as the Penguins used a team-record 48 players.

"I don't care what E.J. says—and I love him to death—but there were obviously machinations going on involving what was going to happen as we got closer to the draft," recalled then-vice president of marketing Tom Rooney.

The Penguins went 3-13 in March, and Johnston had his man. The Penguins finished with 38 points, New Jersey with 41. The Devils openly questioned the Penguins' policies late in the year.

Johnston didn't care. He was ready to draft the man who would save Penguins hockey.

"For once, we control our own destiny," Johnston said at the time. "The impact that Lemieux is going to have on our franchise is something we need. It won't just be the Pittsburgh Penguins; it will be Mario Lemieux and the Pittsburgh Penguins."

BUFFALO STAMPEDE

Marty McSorley witnessed more unusual things than most rookies, because he broke in with the 1983-84 Penguins, one of the worst teams of the modern era.

No sight was more curious than that of Gary Rissling squaring off with Larry Playfair, who often did not play fair.

Rissling stood 5-foot-9, 175 pounds. Playfair was 215. The 6-2 McSorley intervened, and managed to bring Playfair to his knees.

Rissling's eyes lit up.

"Riz looked at it like, 'Oh, boy, now he's my size,'" McSorley said. "He went right after him."

"Not one of my finer moments," said Rissling, who'd been teammates with Playfair in the AHL.

Randy Carlyle quarterbacked the Penguins' most successful power play and was the first defenseman in team history to win the Norris Trophy.
(Photo by Paul Salva, courtesy of the Pittsburgh Penguins)

All three wound up in the penalty box.

"Big Larry leans on the glass, leans over the timekeepers and yells, 'Rissling, I'm going to kill ya,'" McSorley said. "So Riz pulls himself up over the glass—his head is barely over—and starts yelling back. The referee comes over and says, 'All three of you are out of here!' Riz is all smiles. I'm like, 'Oh my goodness.'"

SOUR GRAPES

Don Cherry, also known as "Grapes," would briefly be considered for the Penguins' coaching job in 1980, only a year after he became Enemy No. 1 at the Civic Arena.

Fans hung Cherry's bull terrier, Blue, in effigy, as Cherry's Boston Bruins were dismantling the Penguins in a second-round playoff series.

"I don't mind them wishing me or one of my players to die," Cherry told the *Pittsburgh Press*. "But to say something like that about a defenseless dog like my Blue is senseless."

Colorful GM Baz Bastien died in a tragic car accident. *(Photo courtesy of the Pittsburgh Penguins)*

ALMOST FAMOUS

Seven years after their crushing playoff loss to the New York Islanders, in which they blew a three-games-to-none lead, the Penguins had a chance to return the favor.

The Islanders had achieved great things after the 1975 series. They were the two-time defending Stanley Cup champions going into this first-round, best-of-five series in 1982, but the Penguins shocked the hockey world by erasing a two-games-to-none deficit and forcing Game 5 on Long Island.

There had been a 43-point difference between the teams during the regular season, so it was hard to believe that the Penguins took a 3-1 lead in Game 5 and held it as the clock wound down near the six-minute mark.

The Penguins were riding the wave of a smashing 5-2 victory in Game 4 back in Pittsburgh.

"I'll never forget [announcer] Mike Lange, after we won Game 4, said, 'You gotta believe,'" winger Paul Gardner said. "And when we went to the Island for Game 5 and came out for warm-up, there were huge signs from our fans who'd driven there, saying, 'You gotta believe.' It was a special time."

It was until the Islanders scored twice in the final six minutes, anyway. John Tonelli tied it with 2:21 left when a dump-in banked off the end-boards and popped over the stick of Penguins defenseman Randy Carlyle.

Tonelli picked it up in the slot and beat goaltender Michel Dion, who'd played spectacularly. Twenty-two years later, Carlyle still couldn't believe it.

"It was like God had flipped it over my stick," he said.

"Randy used a big, wide blade, too," teammate Greg Malone said later.

At 6:19 of overtime, Tonelli won it.

Carlyle was directly involved on a series-deciding goal the year before against St. Louis, when a centering pass deflected off his stick to Blues forward Mike Crombeen.

Carlyle, who'd mistakenly gone to the corner on the play, refused to blame bad luck.

"It was a bad brain cramp," he said.

LINESMAN THROWS A CHECK

Somehow, Gary Rissling carved a professional hockey career out of his 5-foot-9, 175-pound frame.

He did so by playing with the energy of a crazed animal.

"He'd stick his chin out to guys and say, 'You can't cut me! You can't cut scar tissue!'" recalled teammate Marty McSorley.

Rissling racked up 832 penalty minutes playing for the Penguins between 1980-85. He remained in the organization until 1987.

Popular Pittsburgh sportscaster Myron Cope announces the winner of the
"Win a Date with Pierre" contest as Pierre Larouche listens. *(Photo courtesy of
the Pittsburgh Penguins)*

His colorful personality made him a natural for television ads. In
one, he chewed a cup to pieces.

In a game one night, he was checked by a lineseman.

"It was in St. Louis, and I was, as usual, on the bench chirp-
ing," Rissling recalled. "There was a linesman—I won't mention his
name—who got tired of it. He came by the boards and ran into me,
bending my arm over the boards. I was hurt, and back then, you
didn't want to tell the trainer, 'I just got injured by the linesman.'"

Rissling fumed. The linesman no doubt realized his mistake.

"The rest of the game, he skated on the other side of the ice,"
Rissling said.

HEARTBREAKER

Former Penguins centerman Greg Malone described it as the sort
of series where you "woke up with sore muscles you didn't even
know you had."

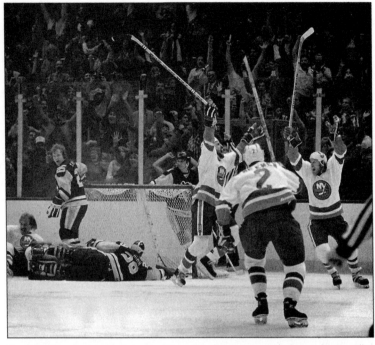

The Islanders broke the Penguins' hearts many times, including John Tonelli's series-winning, overtime goal in 1982. *(Photo courtesy of the Pittsburgh Penguins)*

The Penguins were huge underdogs against the St. Louis Blues in 1981 but forced the best-of-five series to the deciding game in St. Louis. The guy who won it in the second overtime hadn't even played in the first overtime.

Blues forward Mike Crombeen became ill in the third period, then made the Penguins sick all summer with a goal at 5:16 of the second overtime at the raucous Checkerdome in St. Louis.

Penguins goaltender Greg Millen, who would later play for the Blues, drew smiles during the games in St. Louis when he danced in his goal crease to the Budweiser theme song.

Millen also made 48 saves in Game 5, his last game in a Penguins sweater. Malone wound up playing on the same team with Crombeen in Hartford.

"He couldn't even take a puck and flip it on his stick," Malone said, laughing. "I saw him trying it one practice, and I went by and said, 'You scored the goal to beat us?'"

MONEY-BACK GUARANTEE

After his team lost the first two games of a best-of-five, first-round series to the mighty New York Islanders in 1982—by a combined score of 15-3—Penguins owner Edward J. DeBartolo offered fans a refund on tickets purchased for Game 3 and said he would not attend the game.

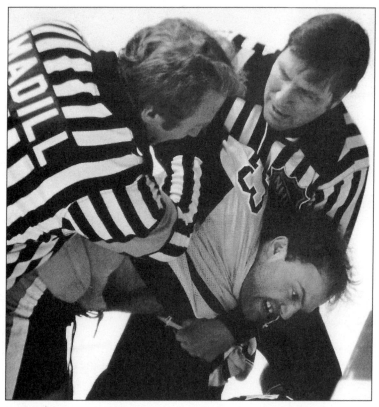

Referees often tried to hold back the gritty Gary Rissling, who once took an elbow from a linesman. *(Photo courtesy of the Pittsburgh Penguins)*

"We took that fairly personally," defenseman Randy Carlyle said. "I can remember [coach] Eddie Johnston coming back and challenging me, specifically, after Game 2. It was a heated conversation. We weren't competing against the defending Stanley Cup champs."

DeBartolo's statement motivated the fans, too. Only about 200 or so took him up on his offer, and when the Penguins took the ice for Game 3, they were greeted with a standing ovation from a boisterous crowd of 14,310.

Intended or not, DeBartolo's pledge had worked to unite everyone against him . . . and in favor of his team.

"It was like people were saying, 'They're our team, and we'll be the ones to criticize them if they need to be criticized. They were our team before you got here, and they'll be our team when you leave,'" recalled Tom Rooney, then the team's vice president of marketing. "I know he didn't do it as a ploy, but it worked."

The Penguins won the next two games before losing a heartbreaking Game 5, in overtime, on Long Island.

FERGY FLIER

The third overtime game in Penguins history produced one of the more memorable finishes—and the fastest victory.

After goalie Denis Heron made the last of his 38 stops in the deciding Game 3 of a playoff series against the Buffalo Sabres, Gregg Sheppard whipped the rebound off the boards, into open ice.

George Ferguson, a.k.a. "The Fergy Flier," snatched it and sped down the left wing at Buffalo's Memorial Auditorium.

By the time his rush was finished, the Penguins had a 4-3 victory.

"I remember it vividly," Ferguson said. "It was such a big goal and such a big upset. Greg Sheppard cleared it, I anticipated it was coming out and took off. I had a lot of speed going down the left wing. A lot of the Sabres were caught napping. I remember going in on the off-wing and cutting to the middle for a better angle."

Everyone remembers Ferguson stuffing a shot past Bob Sauve. It would be the Penguins' last playoff series win until 1989.

THE GREAT TEMPTATION

In 1971, the Penguins began a not-so-grand tradition of trading away their first draft pick. They did it again in 1972, '77, '78, '79, '81 and '83 and had all of three playoff series victories to show for it.

The Pens and the Blues shake hands after the Pens' crushing defeat in a 1981 series. *(Photo courtesy of the Pittsburgh Penguins)*

Yet, several people in the organization wanted general manager Eddie Johnston to deal the No. 1 overall pick in 1984, which was clearly going to be French Canadian sensation Mario Lemieux.

There were some awfully tempting offers. Minnesota GM Lou Nanne, for example, offered all 12 of his team's picks, not that any after the first one or two would have meant much.

"I said, 'Lou, if you [offered all your draft picks] for the next three years in a row, I still wouldn't trade him,'" Johnston said. "If it wasn't for Mario, there wouldn't be a franchise here now. And if we would have traded him, it would have been an injustice to the city of Pittsburgh."

The Quebec Nordiques dangled the three Stastny brothers, Peter, Anton and Marian. The Montreal Canadiens, like Quebec desperate for hometown hero Lemieux, tried to sway Johnston with various combinations of players.

Johnston, himself a Montreal native, was the most popular guy in the league in the days leading up the draft.

And he never considered trading Lemieux. Not for an instant.

Johnston had scouted Lemieux himself and knew a rare talent when he saw one. He had, after all, played for the Boston Bruins when Bobby Orr came along.

Johnston listened to his higher-ups but refused to indulge their wishes.

"I just told them, 'I'm not dealing him,'" Johnston said. "There were some people who were saying we can get a lot of good players, but I remember [owner Edward J. DeBartolo] saying to me later, 'Thank God you didn't listen.'

"This place would be a parking lot."

3

WAITING TO WIN

(1984–1990)

TABLE HOCKEY

Talk about a buzz kill. About 1,500 Penguins fans excitedly watched the 1984 NHL Draft on closed-circuit TV at the Civic Arena, only to see top pick Mario Lemieux, on the advice of his agents, break tradition and refuse to approach the Penguins' table when his name was announced.

Lemieux, embroiled in a contract dispute, also refused to wear a Penguins jersey for publicity photos (he later said he regretted both moves).

Typical Penguins, many fans thought.

"The next day, we were flooded with phone calls from season-ticket holders," recalled then-vice president of marketing Tom Rooney. "They were saying, 'I'll sign when he signs.'"

Within days, Lemieux signed the largest rookie contract in NHL history, worth some $700,000.

A VIEW FOR LEMIEUX

The *New York Times* once called Pittsburgh "the only city with an entrance." There is no hint of a metropolis even as one drives to within a few hundred yards of it, on the Parkway West from the airport.

A hill blocks the spectacular skyline, which dramatically greets visitors as they emerge from the Fort Pitt Tunnel.

Paul Steigerwald, then a Penguins marketer, remembers when Mario Lemieux first laid on eyes on his new kingdom in the summer of 1984. Steigerwald had been dispatched to pick up Lemieux, plus Lemieux's father and agent, at the airport shortly after the NHL Draft.

Lemieux was 18.

"I prepped him for the view, and his eyes lit up when we went through the tunnel," Steigerwald said. "He could understand English, but he didn't want to speak it much. He just nodded his head.

"Even then, he had a touch of royalty about him."

FAST START

It took rookie center Mario Lemieux all of one shift to make an indelible mark on the National Hockey League. On October 11, 1984, at the fabled Boston Garden, he accidentally blocked a point shot by future Hall of Fame defenseman Raymond Bourque, skated in on a breakaway and deked goaltender Pete Peeters out of his jock before tucking the puck into an open net.

First game, first shift, first shot, first goal.

"Pete went one way, Mario went the other," recalled Eddie Johnston, the man who drafted Lemieux. "On the first shift of training camp, he did the same thing. He got the puck, went through the whole team and scored. First exhibition game, same thing.

"So, it didn't surprise me when he did that. But I think everybody else was in awe."

And would be for years to come.

SORRY

Mike Lange's most embarrassing moment as Voice of the Penguins?

Easy: The night he expressed on-air condolences to the family of the supposedly deceased Warren Riefer, events coordinator at the Civic Arena.

Riefer was still alive.

The problem began when arena employee Elaine Heufelder heard from a co-worker about Riefer's "death" and asked Lange if he would mention it during the Penguins' telecast that night.

Riefer was a familiar figure at the arena, busily navigating the halls on a golf cart. He was gravely ill at the time and would die within weeks, but he was watching the game from his hospital bed when Lange mentioned his name.

Mario Lemieux reacts after scoring his first NHL goal—on his first shot—on October 12, 1984, in Boston. Pete Peeters is the goaltender. *(AP/WWP)*

"I said, 'We'll miss him, and we express condolences to family and friends,'" Lange said. "Next day, I get a call. He's not dead. He was watching the broadcast, and he almost lost it he laughed so hard. I think he even sent me a note saying how much he enjoyed it.

"At that time, I made a decision: I would have to see the person in the box to be able to say they had died."

LEMIEUX DEBUT

Ex-Vancouver Canucks winger Gary Lupul had a respectable NHL career but is remembered most for one thing: eating Mario Lemieux's fists.

"My nephews pulled my name up on the Internet, and it shows Mario giving me an uppercut," Lupul told the *Pittsburgh Tribune-Review*. "I played 300 games in the league, and I'm 40th in Canucks history in scoring, and a lot of people only remember that."

How could they forget?

It was a rainy night in Pittsburgh on October 17, 1984, Mario Lemieux's first home game. The Penguins' public relations staff billed it "The Lemieux Debut."

Lemieux set up a goal 18 seconds into what would become a 4-3 victory. Right after that, the 5-foot-9 Lupul started hounding Lemieux, who was seven inches taller.

Lupul slashed Lemieux and pushed him and finally speared him at the three-minute mark.

People questioned whether Lemieux would be able—or at least willing—to protect himself. He answered emphatically. He whipped off his gloves and buried Lupul in a flurry of punches that stunned everyone in the building.

Who expected this? The fans went bonkers.

This was like football!

"Right away, he was a hero to Pittsburgh fans because he was a tough guy, too," recalled Mike Lange, who called the game on television.

"I would say I got in about 10 uppercuts," Lemieux said after the game.

In the other dressing room, an embittered Lupul fired back the only way he could—with words.

"If he plays like that in this league," Lupul said, "he'll never last."

Mario Lemieux proved in his first home game—"The Lemieux Debut"—that he wasn't afraid to drop the gloves, here pounding Vancouver's Gary Lupul. *(Photo courtesy of the Pittsburgh Penguins)*

SNAPPING A JINX

The Penguins had gone 15 years and 42 games (0-39-3) without a victory at the Spectrum in Philadelphia entering their matchup there on February 2, 1989.

It had been so long that their most recent victory occurred with maskless Andy Brown in goal.

Head coach Gene Ubriaco decided to play back-up goaltender Wendell Young over Tom Barrasso, figuring maybe a former Flyer such as Young could help break the streak. (When the Flyers traded

Young the year before, owner Ed Snider said to him, "My fear is that you'll come back to haunt us.")

Others were way more superstitious than Ubriaco. Radio station 3-WS collected good-luck charms that ranged from cakes to old jerseys to women's undergarments.

"A lot of weird stuff," recalled 3-WS sportscaster Tab Douglas, who still has Young's stick from the game. "The most interesting thing a guy gave me was a little piece of yellow plastic. He said, 'I've been carrying that thing around for 10 years as a good luck charm.' It was a piece of a seat from the upper deck in Three Rivers Stadium, where Willie Stargell hit a home run that cracked a seat."

Injured Penguins Randy Cunneyworth and Zarley Zalapaski helped collect the items at a public free-for-all outside the arena. Douglas drove the box of trinkets to Philadelphia and dropped it in the Penguins' dressing room after their morning skate.

Invoking the supernatural as a way to win in Philly was nothing new—forwards Rob Brown and Phil Bourque had jokingly tried hypnosis for a game earlier in the year—but on this day, the madness reached a new level.

Pittsburgh radio hosts Scott Paulsen and Jim Krenn of WDVE-FM did their afternoon show from the Spectrum press box dressed as witch doctors, and Bourque wore his girlfriend's garter belt under his hockey pants.

It worked. Or something did. Young made 39 saves. John Cullen, Bourque, Bob Errey, Troy Loney and Dan Quinn scored the goals in a 5-3 victory.

Somebody suggested to Ubriaco that his team finally got the monkey off its back.

"More like a gorilla," he said.

CRAWL SPACE

When a talented Penguins team got off to a rough start in 1989, fans targeted head coach Gene Ubriaco, who dealt with the criticism creatively.

Ubriaco began walking under the stands to the bench so as to avoid catcalls. He climbed through a small doorway to get to his spot behind the players.

"Yup, he had a little trap door, and I remember him coming out from crawling underneath the bench, wiping all the peanuts off his suit and saying, 'Let's go, guys,'" winger Rob Brown said. "We eventually looked to see what he had to crawl through to get there. It was pretty disgusting."

One night, equipment manager Steve Latin remembered, Ubriaco crawled to his trap door only to find it locked. Ubriaco pounded on the door during the national anthem before somebody finally let him in.

Was it an accident?

"Well, we just kind of left him there for a little bit," Latin said. "He thinks it was an accident."

GREAT TRADE

Former NHL goaltending great Tony Esposito lasted only 106 games as Penguins general manager, but he made an important contribution to the two Stanley Cup championships that occurred shortly after his departure.

Esposito brought Tom Barrasso to Pittsburgh.

"Here's the way I put it," said Wendell Young, one of Barrasso's back-ups. "Mario won the Conn Smythe [as playoff MVP] two years in a row, but Tommy could just as easily have won. There were two key guys on the team: Mario and Tommy."

Esposito sent defenseman Doug Bodger and left winger Darrin Shannon—the No. 4 pick overall in 1988—to Buffalo for Barrasso and a third-round draft choice.

It might have been the greatest trade in Penguins history. Barrasso had won a Vezina Trophy as a 19-year-old in Buffalo and was looking to recapture his mojo.

The Penguins needed a stopper.

"Tony knew goaltenders," said former Penguins president Paul Martha. "And he'd say, 'You can't win a Stanley Cup without a great goalkeeper. That's proven year after year.'"

The Penguins depended heavily on Barrasso, who set an NHL record with a 14-game postseason winning streak. The first 11 victories came in the 1992 playoffs against the New York Rangers, the Boston Bruins and the Chicago Blackhawks.

Barrasso was 16-5 with a 2.82 goals-against average in the playoffs that year, leading the team to its second consecutive Cup. The previous season, he was 12-7 with a 2.60 goals-against average. That included an 8-0 shutout victory at Minnesota in a Cup-clinching Game 6, when the Penguins were outshot 39-28.

Tom Barrasso brought championship-caliber goaltending to Pittsburgh.
(Photo courtesy of the Pittsburgh Penguins)

Young had been acquired before Barrasso, with considerably less fanfare. Coach Gene Ubriaco advised Esposito to acquire Young, who was coming off a great playoff run in the American Hockey League.

Esposito's response: "Who the hell is Wendell Young?"

CHICKEN EGGS

Long before Ville Nieminen, the Penguins had another Finn named Ville. Both made interesting use of the English language.

Ville Siren was a defenseman who came along in 1984, when European players were scarce in the NHL. Veteran defenseman Moe Mantha took Siren under his wing. The two went everywhere together.

Siren struggled to convey his thoughts in English, so whenever Mantha ordered at a restaurant, Siren would say, "Same as him."

One morning in New York, Mantha set Siren free.

"I said to him, 'You're on your own today,'" Mantha recalled. "When the waitress asked him what he wanted, he said, 'I'll have eggs and bacon and toast.'"

And when the waitress asked Siren what kind of eggs he wanted, he said, "Chicken."

FLYING TELEVISION

Former Penguins television analyst Paul Steigerwald couldn't remember the exact date. Understandably so, considering what happened:

A replay monitor dropped from its perch and clipped the side of his head and shoulder, causing a mid-sentence shut down as he and Mike Lange called a game.

"Mike just glanced at me, shook his head in disbelief and continued to call the game as if nothing had happened," Steigerwald said. "Eventually, he told the viewers, 'A TV monitor just fell on Staggy's head,' and asked if I was OK.

"I cracked the obligatory joke about needing a helmet in the booth and went about my work, realizing that I could have been seriously injured if I had been sitting six inches to my right.

"Imagine your 17-inch television landing on your head, and you'll get the picture."

PIERRE CREAMER

Let the record show that Pierre Creamer, in his only season as Penguins coach (1987-88), produced the team's best winning percentage in nine years.

Let it also show that the mostly French-speaking Creamer confused an awful lot of people, including his players.

For proof, refer to the second-last game of the season.

The Penguins needed to win to keep their playoff hopes alive, but Creamer thought his team needed only a tie and failed to pull his goaltender as time wound down in a 6-6 deadlock with the Washington Capitals.

"We were on the bench, and [forward] Dave Hunter was yelling to Pierre, 'We need to win!'" winger Rob Brown recalled. "We were all turning around, saying, 'Are you going to pull our goalie?'

"[Creamer] was calling upstairs and was convinced we needed a tie, but somebody told him that was wrong."

Finally, Creamer called timeout—and proceeded to speak French with star center Mario Lemieux while the other five players on the ice stared blankly at each other.

"We're like, 'Ah, Pierre, we don't speak French,'" Brown said. "I'm sure he said to Mario, 'Go end to end and win the game,' and that's exactly what happened."

Lemieux scored a remarkable goal while falling on his back. The Penguins missed the playoffs, anyway. Gene Ubriaco replaced Creamer after the season.

Brown had another memory of Creamer. It was Brown's first year, and Creamer called him into his office near the end of training camp.

"He said, 'Rob, we like you, but we think you're our No. 6 center; we're going to send you to junior,'" Brown said. "I said, 'I can't go to junior.' He said, 'How old are you?' I said, '19,' which made me too old.

"So he says, 'OK, you'll start the season here.' Well, all righty then."

Brown had 24 goals in 51 games that year, fourth best on the team.

penguique...

eyetique

Mike Lange and Paul Steigerwald had some memorable moments in the broadcast booth. *(Photo courtesy of the Pittsburgh Penguins)*

MAKING A BIKE

Head coach Pierre Creamer was incensed one morning, ex-goaltender Gilles Meloche recalled, and kicked his players off the ice. Creamer ordered them to ride exercise bikes, only his words weren't clear.

GM Eddie Johnston (right) introduces Pierre Creamer, who wore the coaching cap for one unforgettable season. *(Photo courtesy of the Pittsburgh Penguins)*

A French-Canadian, Creamer sometimes mangled his English, especially when he was mad. His exact words to the players that day were, "Go make a bike!"

The players proceeded to draw a bicycle on the chalkboard and head home.

MARKETING MARIO

Bob Berry's arrival as Penguins coach in 1984 coincided with Mario Lemieux's arrival as franchise savior. This wasn't always a good thing, at least not for the marketing department.

Berry was an old-time hockey guy who'd come from Montreal, where no marketing of the local hockey club was necessary.

It was critical in Pittsburgh. Attendance the year before Lemieux arrived was 6,839 per game with exactly zero sellouts. Berry figured a winner would take care of attendance problems.

In the meantime, he didn't have much time—or patience—for promotions.

"We used to battle with Bob all the time about doing things like taking Mario from practice to some grand opening of a Burger King or something," recalled then-vice president of marketing, Tom Rooney, who immediately seized on the fact that Lemieux's last name, in French, means "The Best."

"Mario, at that point in time, didn't know any better."

Everywhere Pittsburghers looked, there was Lemieux. Fans could buy a Mario Lemieux Growth Chart, and *Sports Illustrated* made him do a photo shoot at the Pittsburgh Zoo, where he was photographed among live penguins.

One day, marketing director Paul Steigerwald poked his head into Berry's office to inform him that *Evening Magazine*, a local television show, wanted to bring a live penguin to practice for a photo shoot.

"Well, keep the [expletive] thing away from me," Berry grumbled.

It didn't get any better as the season wore on.

Said Rooney: "We got in more and more trouble."

HEXTALL'S FURY

Rob Brown wasn't even that excited about his goal, because the game was out of hand.

Philadelphia Flyers goalie Ron Hextall was pretty hyped, though.

Brown, known for hot-dog celebrations, had put the Penguins ahead 9-2 in Game 5 of a first-round, best-of-seven series against the hated Flyers. As he went to hug teammate Dan Quinn, he saw Hextall charging his way with his stick raised above his head.

Hextall—the son of former Penguins defenseman Bryan Hextall—seemed intent on decapitating Brown, who wasn't the world's fastest skater but quickly found a new gear. He took a U-turn and sped out of harm's way.

The incident made for one of the more memorable video clips in Penguins history.

"I'll never forget the look on Danny Quinn's face when I skated away from him as he was about to hug me," Brown said. "It was like, 'Where are you going?' It was probably the quickest I've ever skated in my life.

"Whenever I see somebody from Pittsburgh, that's always the thing they ask me about. They'll never forget it. Neither will I."

The goal, incidentally, wound up being important, because the Flyers stormed back before losing, 10-7. Philadelphia won the last two games of the series to hand the Penguins yet another crushing playoff defeat.

CIRCUS PERFORMERS

The Penguins began the 1986-87 season by winning seven consecutive games. The giddiness soon wore off, and by March, Coach Bob Berry was ready to strangle somebody.

Namely, his players.

Berry let loose March 5 after a 7-2 loss at home to the Toronto Maple Leafs. It came two days after an 8-1 win at Quebec. His postgame tirade took an immediate place of prominence among all-time Penguin meltdowns.

"Win one, 8-1, lose one, 7-2—easy come, easy go," Berry fumed. "That's the [expletive] attitude we had tonight. They don't have the [expletive] intestinal fortitude. Big shots. In the back door, put the [expletive] show on, back out on the bus, go somewhere else, just like circus performers.

"They tell everybody they're professional hockey players. They might be [expletive] hockey players, but they're not very [expletive] professional.

"That's all I've got to say."

VALIANT EFFORT

On Valentine's Day, 1990, Mario Lemieux was pierced to the heart. Lemieux had picked up at least one point in each of the previous 46 games, the second-longest streak in NHL history behind Wayne Gretzky's 51.

Lemieux fought crippling back pain during much of the streak. It finally forced him out of a game against the New York Rangers in the second period.

"It's tough to accept," he said afterward. "But that's the way it goes."

Earlier in the season, equipment manager Steve Latin had carpenters make a special contraption—similar to something one would

Coach Bob Berry once labeled his team "circus performers."
(Photo courtesy of the Pittsburgh Penguins)

find in a shoestore—that allowed Lemieux to tie his skates without bending his back.

"He was having so many problems just putting his skates on," Latin recalled. "Just standing up was a chore."

MAGIC STICK

Things were not going well for right winger Ron Duguay in 1986. A one-time 40-goal scorer, his career was in decline, and he was mired in a lengthy slump.

Former teammate Bob Errey picks up the story from there.

"He hadn't scored in a dozen games or so," Errey said. "We were in New York and went to this bar in Manhattan. He sees one of his sticks on the wall—one he'd scored a hat trick with 10 years earlier with the Rangers—and grabs it off the wall."

Duguay used the stick the next night against the Islanders. Needless to say, he scored.

"Somebody dumped it in on the left boards. It hit a partition, and the goalie went back to play it, but it came out in front," Errey said, laughing. "Doogs was all alone. He put it in the wide-open net. He was dancing around.

"After the game, his stick representative was there, and Doogs had them make a few dozen sticks in that exact same pattern."

Duguay's luck didn't last. He had only 11 goals in 53 games with the Penguins and bounced around the NHL for a few more years before playing in the minors and eventually becoming a coach.

CRAIG PATRICK

Born of royal hockey lineage—a member of the famous Patrick family—Craig Patrick was an assistant coach under Herb Brooks when the United States won a miraculous gold medal in 1980.

Patrick went on to produce 11 consecutive Penguins playoff teams and won two Stanley Cups after he was hired as the team's general manager on December 5, 1989.

But he started out like any other kid who loves sports.

If you walked into Patrick's bedroom in Wellesley, Massachusetts, around 1955, you'd find shoeboxes filled with baseball cards, stacked halfway up the walls.

If you walked outside, you might find Patrick firing a tennis ball against the garage. He was pretending to be his favorite team, the Detroit Tigers (he was born in Detroit).

He aimed between the windows of his parents' bedroom and waited for the ball to bounce back. If it eluded him, it was recorded as a single, double, or triple, depending on where it landed.

If it bounced over the wall behind him, it was a home run. Only a hard pitch could result in a homer, but even back then, Patrick found a way to make his team win.

"When the Tigers were up," he said, "I always threw a little harder."

If you could peak into one of his elementary school classes, you might see Patrick working at his desk. The assignments varied, the theme did not.

Always hockey.

Patrick's grandfather, Lester, already was a renowned NHL figure, one of the original builders of the game. Craig's father, Lynn,

Craig Patrick sits dejectedly in the media interview room on March 31, 1990, just after telling reporters his team would never miss the playoffs again, as it did that night on Buffalo's overtime goal. *(Photo by James M. Kubus/ Pittsburgh Tribune-Review)*

managed the Boston Bruins. Craig Patrick loved to watch games at the old Boston Garden. He sat in the same seats every time.

Not that any of this mattered to his teachers, who were concerned about his hockey obsession. They would send him home with written complaints pinned to his chest.

These were not anonymous teachers, either. One was the sister of hockey legend Art Ross, another the sister of Hall of Fame goalie Roy Worters.

"They complained, too," Patrick said.

CLASSIC TAPE

Little did Tracy Luppe know that when he arrived at the Civic Arena on New Year's Eve, 1988, he would become a part of hockey history.

A small part, to be sure, but a part nonetheless.

Mario Lemieux celebrates one of his five goals against New Jersey on New Year's Eve, 1988, the night he became the only player in NHL history to score every type of goal in a game. *(Photo courtesy of the Pittsburgh Penguins)*

Mario Lemieux that night became the only player in NHL history to score each type of goal—even-strength, power-play, short-handed, penalty shot and empty-net—in the same game.

Lemieux's last goal of the night (the empty-netter) appeared to occur slightly after time had elapsed in an 8-6 victory over the New Jersey Devils, but who wanted to spoil such a celebratory moment on New Year's Eve?

Certainly not Luppe, who, for the first time, taped Lemieux's sticks before the game that night. Luppe had been working for the team for four years.

"Mario said, 'Hey, you want to tape my sticks?'" Luppe recalled in 2004. "I'm like, 'What?' He says, 'Yeah, you want to tape my sticks?' Well, he goes out and gets five goals five different ways. Needless to say, I'm still doing them today."

When new players join the Penguins, they take note of the fact that Luppe prepares each of Lemieux's four sticks before every game.

"A few guys are like, 'Hey, tape my sticks; see if it rubs off,'" Luppe said.

THE "OTHER" LEMIEUX

Alain Lemieux, Mario's younger brother, played exactly one game for the Penguins, during the 1986-87 season.

Mario Lemieux wore No. 66, of course, which led equipment man John Doolan to jokingly offer Alain Lemieux No. 33 when he joined the team.

"I teased him that he was only half as good as his brother," Doolan said.

Alain Lemieux wore No. 11 that night. His older brother was injured and did not play.

SINGE-ING THE BLUES

By the end of the 2003-04 season, Mario Lemieux had played only 26 games in 16 seasons against the St. Louis Blues but had somehow managed 25 goals and 58 points.

What's more, he had recorded games of two goals, three goals, four goals, five goals, seven points and eight points against St. Louis—and that didn't include the 1988 All-Star Game at St. Louis, when he scored three goals and set up three others.

"Ridiculous," said Lemieux's former teammate, Ian Moran. "I just get really disappointed when he gets more goals in one game than I get in a season."

There's more.

Lemieux recorded his first career hat trick against St. Louis (a four-goal effort on New Year's Eve, 1985), and the Blues are the only team that pops up on his personal-record list for goals, assists, and points.

He scored five goals three times, including once against the Blues on March 26, 1996, in an 8-4 victory in Wayne Gretzky's only appearance at the Civic Arena in a Blues sweater.

Lemieux dished out six assists three times, once against the Blues (October 15, 1988, in a 9-2 victory at the Civic Arena). That was one of the two eight-point games in his career.

Any explanation for this phenomenon?

"No," Lemieux said. "None whatsoever."

COFFEY BREAK

Tom McMillan was a beat writer covering the Penguins when they acquired defenseman Paul Coffey from Edmonton on November 24, 1987.

McMillan had watched the team since childhood and later became its vice president of communications and marketing. He'd never seen anything like Coffey, a three-time Stanley Cup winner who had three assists in his home debut, as the Penguins roared back from a 4-0 deficit in the final 25 minutes to defeat the Quebec Nordiques, 6-4, in overtime.

"The first time he got the puck and skated, you couldn't believe a Penguin was skating that fast," McMillan said. "At that point, you got the sense they could actually be good. That started the avalanche of all these great players coming here.

"Before that, it was really only Mario."

GM Eddie Johnston engineered the deal, sending Craig Simpson, Dave Hannan, and Moe Mantha to Edmonton for Dave Hunter, Wayne Van Dorp, and Coffey, a three-time Stanley Cup winner who was mired in a contract holdout at the time.

Suddenly, Lemieux had a player who could create space, feed him pinpoint passes, and quarterback the left point on the power play.

The rest of the league was in trouble.

Defenseman Paul Coffey wore extra-small skates and dull blades—and, man, could he fly. *(Photo courtesy of the Pittsburgh Penguins)*

LINE DANCING

When former Penguins winger Luc Robitaille said a fire hydrant could score 40 goals on Mario Lemieux's line, everybody knew it was a gross exaggeration.

No way Lemieux could coax more than 20 goals out of a hydrant.

But the guys who have played on his lines will tell you that he took their games to never-imagined heights. They'll also tell you it was as much a challenge as it was a treat.

If it were easy to mesh with Lemieux's greatness, he wouldn't have gone through linemates like underwear his first several years. A guy can't just walk off the street and play a duet with George Winston or act a scene with Al Pacino in front of 17,000 people.

"You have to have a guy who's confident in his abilities, who has some self-worth," said Penguins radio analyst Bob Errey, a longtime Lemieux linemate.

Skating with Lemieux is the opportunity of a lifetime. Ask Warren Young, who scored 40 goals as a 28-year-old rookie journeyman, or Terry Ruskowski, who, at 31, had a career-best 26 goals next to Lemieux.

Ask Markus Naslund, who had 15 points in his first 85 NHL games, then scored 52 in 66 games with Lemieux.

Ask Jaromir Jagr, who had a personal-best 62 goals on Lemieux's right in 1995-96. Ask Errey, who had a career-best 26 goals in 1988-89, or Rob Brown, who had a career-high 115 points as a 20-year-old.

Lemieux's best line early in his career had Brown on the right and Errey on the left. In 1992-93, he formed a dynamic trio with Kevin Stevens and Rick Tocchet, then with Jagr and Ron Francis.

Early on, one of Lemieux's lines saw him skate with Ruskowski and Doug Shedden.

"[Lemieux] would say, 'Give me the puck and go to the net and keep your stick on the ice,'" Shedden recalled. "OK, that's easy enough."

How long did it take Brown to adjust?

"One game, because I wanted to stay there bad," he said. "I wanted to make sure I was ready. I remember we were driving back from the airport one day, and Ken Schinkel, the assistant GM, told me I'd be on Mario's line. I had a smile on my face the rest of the day."

JOHNNY ON THE SPOT

Through good times and bad, a familiar voice rang through the rafters at Penguins games.

The late public address announcer John Barbero, a bespectacled former high school English teacher (later a principal), and one-time radio voice of the American Basketball Association's Pittsburgh Pipers, started playing games with players' names early in his career.

Some players didn't like it.

"I dragged out the Z's on Zarley Zalapski, and he told me he was embarrassed," said Barbero, who started working games in the early 1970s. "He asked me not to do it anymore."

One day in the late 1980s, TV announcer Mike Lange said to Barbero, "Why don't you do something with Mario?"

Next game, Barbero belted out what became his signature call: "Pittsburgh goal scored by No. 66, Mario Lemiuewwwwwwww!"

Fans loved it.

How did Lemieux feel?

"He never said a word," Barbero said, "so I assumed he liked it."

MUSIC TO THEIR EARS

Before ear-splitting acid rock made its way into hockey arenas, organists filled the breaks in action. Penguins organist Vince Lascheid was one of the best. His creative and well-timed ditties tickled the home fans and sometimes infuriated opponents and referees.

When gritty Penguins forward Pat Hickey went to the penalty box, Lascheid would crank out a Cole Porter tune called, "I've Got You Under My Skin."

When the referees came out before the game, Lascheid was liable to play "Three Blind Mice."

"Sometimes the songs were very poor," Lascheid said, "but at least it was something."

Other Lascheid classics:

- "The Godfather Theme Song"—off-key—directed at Boston Bruins superstar Phil Esposito.
- "Tommy" for Penguins goalie Tom Barrasso.
- "Anchors Aweigh" for Penguins enforcer Bob "Battleship" Kelly.
- Theme from the TV show "Bonanza" for fighter Steve Durbano.
- The Maxwell House jingle for defenseman Paul Coffey.

- "The Night Chicago Died" when the Penguins beat the Chicago Blackhawks.
- "Give My Regards To Broadway" when they beat the New York Rangers.
- "The Night The Lights Went Out In Georgia" when they beat the Atlanta Flames.

The NHL took offense to Lascheid playing "Three Blind Mice" and ordered him to quit, but he still sneaked it in every once a while "just to see what would happen."

Once, referee Paul Stewart called the press box to complain.

One of Lascheid's early classics was the homemade chant, "Let's Go Pronovost!" in honor of Penguins star Jean Pronovost. It was the counter-chant to Buffalo Sabres fans yelling, "Let's Go Buffalo!"

Sabres fans used to travel to Pittsburgh by the busload, making for a charged atmosphere at the Civic Arena.

"The Pronovost thing started when I was driving through the Liberty Tunnels one night," said Lascheid, who passed away in 2009. "I started with my horn—Da-da-dadada. Lo and behold, everybody started honking their horns, too. It was a lot of fun."

MANTHA'S HOT TUB

In the mid-1980s, defenseman Moe Mantha had the most popular house on the team, complete with indoor shuffleboard, a bowling alley and a backyard hot tub.

Mantha recalls that youngsters Mario Lemieux, Doug Bodger, and Roger Belanger—the team's top three draft picks from 1984—would sometimes come over to sit in the hot tub and smoke cigars.

"Little 19-year-old rookies smoking cigars in the hot tub," Mantha recalled, laughing. "I've got pictures of it. If I ever need a job, I might call Mario and blackmail him, the skinny little runt."

STAR OF STARS

The NHL All-Star Game came to Pittsburgh on January 21, 1990, and it became the Mario Lemieux Show precisely 21 seconds after the opening faceoff. That was when Lemieux scored one of his four goals, joining Wayne Gretzky as the only NHL players to accomplish the feat to that point. In only his sixth season, Lemieux was named All-Star Game MVP for an unprecedented third time.

CRAZY MAN

Rob Brown was plain nuts when he played junior hockey. He would write messages to opposing players on the tape of his stick. He would goof off against inferior opponents.

And he would go to team parties dressed in his coach's pants.

That's right, Brown and his friend Mark Recchi, another future Penguin, each put their whole body in one of 500-pound coach Ken Hitchcock's pant legs. The two simultaneously shared one of Hitchcock's jackets, too. That's how they walked into a Kamloops team party together in 1986.

Hitchcock eventually lost weight and became an accomplished NHL coach.

Brown, too, experienced a remarkable transformation. Four seasons removed from scoring 115 points on a line with Mario Lemieux, he had no NHL contract and wound up in the minors. He worked his way back to the NHL several years later and re-invented himself as a checker under Penguins coach Kevin Constantine.

HIRING PATRICK

Craig Patrick was on the Penguins' radar more than a year before he was hired.

"I tried to get him to the Penguins earlier," said ex-team president Paul Martha. "I met with him a couple of times at LaGuardia Airport."

Patrick had been fired by the New York Rangers, but the Penguins hired Tony Esposito in April, 1988, on the orders of owner Edward J. DeBartolo. When Esposito was fired in December of 1989, Martha knew who to call.

"I'd done my homework," he said. "A lot of people felt Craig Patrick was the upcoming guy. I was able to convince Mr. [Edward] DeBartolo that Craig Patrick was really the right choice."

WINNER'S CIRCLE

Goaltender Wendell Young made Penguins history when he stopped 39 shots to help break the team's 15-year jinx at the Spectrum in Philadelphia. That wasn't his greatest feat, though.

This was: He is the only player to have won each of the following four championships in North American hockey: the Stanley Cup (Penguins, 1991 and '92); the American Hockey League's Calder Cup (Hershey Bears, 1988); the Canadian Major Junior's Memorial Cup (Kitchener Rangers, 1982); and the International Hockey League's Turner Cup (Chicago Wolves, 1998, 2000).

Nobody can equal the record, because the International League is extinct.

"It's an amazing thing with the little bit of talent I had," Young said.

His luck didn't stop when he joined the Wolves, who joined the AHL, as the executive director of team relations. The team won the Calder Cup in 2002, giving Young yet another ring.

WREGGET'S GAME 7

A smoker at the time, Philadelphia Flyers goaltender Ken Wregget was dying for a cigarette before Game 7 of a 1989 playoff series against the Penguins.

Wregget and Flyers trainer Kurt Mundt used to leave a pack of matches in a hidden spot at every arena so that when they went for a smoke, they had an easy light.

On this particular morning at the Civic Arena, Wregget had just been informed that starting goalie Ron Hextall couldn't play because of a bad knee.

Few favored the Flyers, playing a back-up goalie against the turbo-charged Penguins, who'd won Game 5 at the Civic Arena, 10-7.

Wregget, who would join the Penguins three years later, remembers waiting anxiously for the game to start.

"The nerves were phenomenal," he said. "I remember the hotel room, trying to sleep, seeing the big silver dome [of the Civic Arena] outside of my window. It was kind of ominous."

When Wregget finally got to the game, he was a basket case. Mundt calmed him down.

"He said, 'This is the stuff you dream about your whole life; you shouldn't be scared about it. Just relax and have fun,'" Wregget recalled. "I thought, 'He's right.'"

Wregget stoned the Penguins in a 4-1 victory.

DRAFTING JAGR

The Penguins caught a break when the Philadelphia Flyers fired general manager Bobby Clarke on the eve the 1990 NHL Draft. Clarke coveted a talented Czechoslovakian winger named Jaromir Jagr.

So did Penguins GM Craig Patrick, who had seen Jagr at the World Championships, skating on the Czechs' third line with future NHLers Bobby Holik and Robert Reichel.

"We were hoping we would get him," Patrick said. "But we were real worried."

Other teams had their own concerns about Jagr. Some feared he wouldn't be able to get out of Czechoslovakia. Others were said to be leery of European players.

The Vancouver Canucks, drafting second overall in their home arena, opted for a Czech who had defected to North America—Petr Nedved—after the Quebec Nordiques took Owen Nolan with the first pick.

The Detroit Red Wings took Keith Primeau third, followed by the Flyers. Jagr later recalled his heart pounding as the Flyers prepared to announce their selection. He thought he was headed to Philadelphia, but the Flyers took forward Mike Ricci.

That left the Penguins to snag Jagr, who would be become one of the most dynamic offensive talents in NHL history.

"He was, by far, the best prospect," said Penguins head scout Greg Malone "We had to take him."

Patrick recalled that Jagr wanted to come to North America immediately, but to clinch the deal, Patrick flew Jagr and his parents to Pittsburgh after the draft.

"Craig showed him the city, let his parents see it so they would know what they were getting into," Malone said. "The plan was to get him here as quick as possible. At the end of the week, his parents were comfortable with letting him come."

The Penguins also had to pay Jagr's Czech team in Kladno $200,000.

Years later, a reporter asked Patrick the following question: "If somebody had asked you privately whether you were confident you'd get Jagr, what would you have said?"

Patrick's answer revealed plenty about his management style.

"I wouldn't have said anything," he said. "I wouldn't have let anybody know that's what we wanted."

PARTY TIME

When Jaromir Jagr first arrived in Pittsburgh, immediately after the 1990 NHL Draft, Penguins general manager Craig Patrick threw a small party at his apartment. Patrick invited several local Czechs and told Jagr that he could pick a family with whom to live.

Jagr, in his self-titled autobiography, remembered a late-arriving guest stealing the show. It was Mario Lemieux.

"Mario came up to me, extended his hand and said, 'If you need anything, you can always come to me. I was in the exact same situation you are now when I came to Pittsburgh speaking only French, and I still remember how hard it was. So, don't worry, I know the problems you'll be having, and I know how you're feeling. I'm ready to help you any time,'" Jagr recounted. "I had my picture taken with Mario that night, and to this day, whenever I look at that photograph, I remember what Mario said to me."

It was soon discovered that in jumbling the letters to Jaromir, one could create a rather appropriate anagram: Mario Jr.

HEY SONG

The expansion Colorado Rockies introduced the familiar "Hey Song" to the National Hockey League in the mid-1970s, but it had virtually disappeared from sports arenas before the Penguins revived it during a 1989 playoff series against the Philadelphia Flyers.

The familiar Gary Glitter song—actually titled "Rock & Roll, Part 2"—has since become an anthem of sorts in professional sports venues.

Former Penguins marketer Tinsy Labrie remembered her brother introducing her to the song. Chase Edmondson, who was in charge of music at the arena, liked it and agreed to play it.

Fans loved it.

Edmondson came up with another popular idea during the Stanley Cup years in 1991 and '92. When the Penguins went on a power play, he would play the theme to the movie *Jaws*. Fans would then wave yellow placards picturing shark fins.

THE PROMISE

Nobody was surprised when the Penguins added another heartbreaking chapter to their history on the final day of the 1989-90 season.

Needing a victory to beat the Buffalo Sabres, who'd been eliminated from the playoffs, the Penguins blew it when Sabres defenseman Uwe Krupp beat Tom Barrasso from the left point in overtime.

After the game, a reporter suggested to new Penguins general manager Craig Patrick—also the team's interim coach—that this was typical of the hard-luck Penguins.

"That's going to change," Patrick snapped.

He went on to say that missing the playoffs "would never happen again."

On June 12 of that year, Patrick hired Bob Johnson as his new coach and Scotty Bowman as director of player development and recruitment.

Suddenly, the Penguins had the most feared management group in the NHL.

They would make the playoffs each of the next 11 years and win two Stanley Cups.

4
GLORY DAYS
(1991–1996)

HOW DO YOU LIKE US NOW?

Lovable losers for much of their first 24 years, the Penguins gained instant respect on June 12, 1990, when general manager Craig Patrick hired "Badger" Bob Johnson as coach and Scotty Bowman as director of player development.

Suddenly, the Penguins had three of the most respected names in hockey running their team.

Johnson's rampant optimism would help to transform the culture of hockey in Pittsburgh, and Bowman was the winningest coach in NHL history. He'd been working as an analyst with *Hockey Night in Canada* but was enticed to come to Pittsburgh because of Patrick, who called his new group "the best management team in the NHL."

Others took note.

"A pretty impressive front-end team," remarked Edmonton Oilers GM Glen Sather.

BADGER BOB

The Penguins were a fragile bunch when "Badger" Bob Johnson took the coaching reins in June of 1990.

New general manager Craig Patrick had phoned the 59-year-old Johnson the previous December from the Met Center in Minneapolis.

Johnson had been out of the NHL for three years but immediately said yes when Patrick asked if he'd be interested in coaching again.

Craig Patrick introduces his impressive new management team—coach Bob Johnson and director of player development, Scotty Bowman—on June 12, 1990. (Photo by James M. Kubus/Pittsburgh Tribune-Review)

"Badger" Bob—the nickname came from his days coaching the Wisconsin Badgers—could not join the team until the following season because of obligations to USA Hockey, an entity with which Patrick was intimately familiar.

Patrick had been Herb Brooks' assistant coach with the 1980 US Olympic Team that produced the Miracle on Ice (Johnson's son, Mark, was a star player on that team and later played for the Penguins).

Turning the Penguins into a champion would require a miracle of its own.

The team was coming off a season in which it was eliminated from playoff contention in its final regular-season game in overtime. It was one of many tortuous endings the franchise had suffered in its first 24 years.

Beginnings were often quite painful, too.

"We were teetering," winger Phil Bourque recalled. "We didn't know if we were going to be good or stink."

And they weren't sure what to make of the quirky Johnson, either.

"He was just such a character," defenseman Larry Murphy said. "When I first met him, he gave me this list of top 10 foods. He says, 'I want you to have this.' I remember the banana being No. 1. That sticks out in my mind."

• • •

One of Johnson's first moves was to hold training camp in Vail, Colorado.

Initially, players were bummed. There was nowhere to go, and the altitude made for rough training.

This was part of Johnson's plan.

"For the first few days, guys were puking over the boards because of the altitude," Bourque said. "They were just dying. But after we settled in with the atmosphere and everything, it definitely helped us with our conditioning."

Players became closer because they were virtually forced to spend time together. They went mountain biking and hiking and hung out at night.

Eight months later, they would still be hanging out—at a raucous Stanley Cup celebration at the Met Center in Minneapolis, the same place where Craig Patrick had first contacted "Badger" Bob Johnson.

• • •

Johnson's players loved him because he always had their best interests in mind. This was never truer than during the final game of the 1990-91 season, when the New York Rangers couldn't figure out why the Penguins' bench was so enthusiastic late in a meaningless, 6-3 Rangers victory.

The Penguins had clinched a playoff spot and had nothing at stake that day at Madison Square Garden. Not as a team, anyway. Certain players had contract bonuses on the line.

Late in the game, Johnson shouted to his players on the bench: "Anybody have any bonuses for points or goals?"

Randy Gilhen needed a goal for a $20,000 bonus, so Johnson repeatedly sent him on the ice. In the final minute, Gilhen went out on a power play and scored.

"It was the first time I ever played the power play there," Gilhen recalled. "The greatest thing about Badger was that he instilled so much confidence in the guys. He had you believing you could do anything."

• • •

Never one to adhere to convention, Johnson had his players work out in a hotel ballroom the morning of a 1991 playoff game in Boston.

Whether he was working with NHL players or Pee Wees, "Badger" Bob Johnson loved to teach. *(Photo courtesy of the Pittsburgh Penguins)*

He was eager to test a new breakout.

"He used pucks on the floor," defenseman Larry Murphy recalled. "We were wearing street clothes, and guys were swinging around behind the chairs, working on the breakout. There was never a dull moment back then."

• • •

In five years coaching the Calgary Flames, Johnson came close but did not win a Stanley Cup, so he knew it was the opportunity of a lifetime going into Game 6 of the 1991 final in Minneapolis, the city where he was born.

Veteran forward Joe Mullen, whom Johnson brought to Pittsburgh, remembered seeing Johnson and his wife, Martha, in the corridors before the game.

"They said, 'You have a Cup already. We need this one,'" Mullen said. "I said, 'We'll get it.'"

FLAT ON HIS BACK

All the hope the Penguins carried into the 1990-91 season seemed to disappear during a preseason road trip to Houston, where Mario Lemeiux's back pain literally dropped him to his knees.

Lemieux was coming off surgery to repair a herniated disk. It was discovered the next day that he had a rare disc-space infection. He would lay flat on his back for the next three months and would miss the first 50 games.

"It was a difficult time, lying there on my back, knowing I had an infection that was very serious and could attack my bones and spine," Lemieux recalled in his autobiography, *The Final Period*. "I tell you, I did a lot of thinking."

He began skating in early January. His eventual comeback came to symbolize a season in which the Penguins habitually rose from their backs to snatch victory from defeat. They lost Game 1 in each of their four playoff series but rebounded to win the series every time.

WINNERS ABOARD

Prior to the 1990-91 season, general manager Craig Patrick added a couple of veteran Stanley Cup winners to his roster. Plucky winger

Joe Mullen came from Calgary, and battle-tested center Bryan Trottier came from the New York Islanders, where he'd won four Cups.

"Badger" Bob Johnson loved Mullen, whom he'd brought to Calgary when Johnson coached the Flames.

Patrick and Johnson sold Trottier on a limited role.

"[Johnson] said, 'I'll use the hell out of you in the playoffs,'" Trottier remembered. "That made the decision real easy."

Still, Trottier had been a franchise player, so he struggled with a bit role.

"There were some tense meetings between Bob and I, but it worked out perfectly. He did play the hell out of me in the playoffs. I was out there in the last minute all the time."

THE TRADE

The Hockey News predicted the Hartford Whalers would win the March 4, 1991 trade in which center Ron Francis and defensemen Ulf Samuelsson and Grant Jennings were shipped to the Penguins for center John Cullen, defenseman Zarley Zalapski, and winger Jeff Parker.

Two months later, the Penguins looked like the winners, because they were the ones parading with the Stanley Cup—thanks largely to Francis and Samuelsson.

Ironically, the Whalers general manager at the time was Eddie Johnston, who'd been the Penguins GM in 1984, when the team drafted Mario Lemieux.

Johnston later said he was under extreme pressure from Whalers management to trade Francis, who'd been stripped of his captaincy.

Penguins general manager Craig Patrick wound up with a future Hall of Famer in Francis and the sort of rugged defenseman the Penguins desperately needed in Samuelsson.

Winless in five games the day of the trade, the Penguins promptly won four in a row and nine of 14 to finish the regular season.

They rolled all the way to their first Stanley Cup. The timing and immediate payoff made it the most dramatic trade in team history.

• • •

Samuelsson endeared himself to the Civic Arena faithful in his very first game, a 4-1 victory over Vancouver. Eventually, fans would chant "Ulf! Ulf! Ulf!" every time he touched the puck.

A city filled with Steelers fans, Pittsburgh loved physical defense.

"So many of the plays I was making before were appreciated by teammates, but never the crowd," Samuelsson said. "To be appreciated for the work you're doing—breaking up plays and hitting—is very special."

At 6-foot-1, 205 pounds, Samuelsson wore a pair of oversized shoulder pads and spent much of his time torturing top forwards such as Boston's Cam Neely. People called Samuelsson a linebacker on skates—and he'd do anything to win a game.

"I'm glad he's on our side," Mario Lemieux said.

Sports Illustrated once did a story on Samuelsson called "Mr. Dirty."

"Even my mother says I'm a dirty player," Samuelsson said.

He finished in the NHL's all-time top 20 in penalty minutes with 2,453.

THE SAVE

"Badger" Bob Johnson had a feeling he'd need back-up goalie Frank Pietrangelo in the 1991 playoffs. That is why he gave Pietrangelo two late-season starts.

But even Johnson couldn't have predicted how big a role Pietrangelo would play in the franchise's first Stanley Cup championship.

The Penguins barely made it out of the first round. They trailed the New Jersey Devils, three games to two, going into Game 6 in New Jersey and were without their best defenseman, Paul Coffey (scratched cornea), and their starting goaltender, Tom Barrasso (bruised shoulder).

Goaltender Wendell Young was injured, too, leaving Bruce Racine—who had never played an NHL game—as Pietrangelo's back up.

Before the game, Johnson told Racine: "No matter what, you're not going in. Don't worry."

The rest of the Penguins had plenty to worry about when New Jersey looked to tie the score 2-2 on a power play late in the first period.

Actually, Penguins equipment manager Steve Latin thought the Devils had tied it when forward Peter Stastny flicked a loose puck toward an open net. Pietrangelo had tried to cover the puck, but John MacLean poked it to Stastny.

Frank Pietrangelo makes "The Save" against New Jersey's Peter Stastny in the '91 playoffs. *(Photo courtesy of the Pittsburgh Penguins)*

"All I did was look up at the scoreboard on the side of the arena and look for them to click it," Latin said.

Several Devils players threw their sticks in the air to celebrate, Pietrangelo noticed as he watched the tape later, and Devils fans stood to cheer.

Prematurely, as it turned out.

Pietrangelo lunged to his left and miraculously snagged the puck. It came to be known simply as "The Save" in Pittsburgh hockey lore.

"It was a goal, more or less," Pietrangelo recalled. "It was a bang-bang play, and I made a reaction save. Maybe it gave everyone a lift, like, 'Hey, maybe this is meant to be—maybe we can get it to Game 7.'"

Defenseman Peter Taglianetti was on the ice when it happened. He punched Stastny in the back of the head after the whistle.

"When we went back for a line change, it was like, 'My god, what just happened?'" Taglianetti said. "We knew we dodged a bullet."

The Penguins held on for a 4-3 victory, and Pietrangelo won Game 7, 4-0, before a roaring crowd at the Civic Arena.

Barrasso returned for the next series, but Pietrangelo had carved his place in franchise history. He was doing commercials that summer.

More than a decade later, he became a player agent in Toronto.

"I get asked about the save so many times it's unbelievable," Pietrangelo said. "I'm honored. I really am. And every day I get asked, 'Can I please look at your ring?'"

• • •

Luckily for the Penguins, video replay was not in use during their 1990-91 playoff series against New Jersey. Game 6 of that series is remembered mostly for "The Save," but an equally important near-miss occurred near the end of the second period, when the referee ruled that Devils forward Laurie Boschman kicked the puck into the net. Replays showed that after the puck hit Boschman's skate, it hit his stick, which would have made the goal legal and tied the score going into the third period.

STAR SEARCH

Mario Lemieux, Tom Barrasso, and company weren't the only stars on Civic Arena ice during the early 1990s. A blonde-haired, blue-eyed teenager from Pittsburgh's north suburbs turned heads when she belted out the national anthem on a handful of occasions.

It wasn't until years later, however, that the little girl's name—Christina Aguilera—would be recognized around the world.

BEHIND THE MIKE

Mike Lange's distinctive calls—his first in Pittsburgh was "Great Balls of Fire!"—endeared him to Penguins fans. His calm but entertaining style on television made him a welcome guest in living rooms all over Western Pennsylvania starting in 1979, when Penguins games went from radio, exclusively, to simulcast.

During the Penguins' Stanley Cup years, Lange would exclaim, "Elvis has just left the building!" when a victory was assured (and a fan dressed as Elvis actually would get up and leave the arena at home games).

Great Balls of Fire! Mike Lange is inducted into the broadcasters wing of the Hockey Hall of Fame in 2001. *(Photo by James M. Kubus/Pittsburgh Tribune-Review)*

Lange, a Sacramento, California, native, began with the Penguins in 1974 calling games on radio. He says three of his sayings generated the biggest fan response.

Here's the story behind each:

1. "Scratch my back with a hacksaw" came from a security guard in a Pittsburgh-area shopping mall. "I was going to do a commercial, and I couldn't find the office," Lange said. "He said, 'It's way back in the corner.' Then he said, 'Do you take phrases?' I said, 'Sure.' He wrote it down, and the minute he wrote it down, I thought, 'It's over.' I knew it would work."

2. "He beat him like a rented mule" came from a stockbroker friend. "I called him one day on the phone and asked him how his day went, and he said, 'They're beating me like a rented mule,'" Lange said. During a game in the 2003-04 season, Lange altered the call when the Penguins scored a goal against ex-teammate Johan "Moose" Hedberg. Said Lange, "They beat him like a rented Moose!"

3. "Buy Sam a drink and get his dog one, too." Lange overheard this in a bar one night. "A guy walked in and sat down, and that's exactly what he said."

PETER PAN

Defenseman Peter Taglianetti wasn't sure if he could continue playing in a first-round playoff series against the New Jersey Devils in 1991. "Tags" had a case of lace bite, which meant he had a deep bruise in the spot where he flexed his foot and tied his skates.

"Terribly painful," he said.

When word of the problem reached the press, the U.S. and Canadian ski teams offered help. They sent NASA-produced, space-age foam that had worked with skiers' lace bite.

It didn't work with Taglianetti's.

Peanut butter did.

Penguins trainer Skip Thayer remembered a player on the Chicago Blackhawks, Al Secord, using a plastic baggie filled with peanut butter to alleviate lace-bite pain. Secord placed the baggie under the flap of his skate.

Taglianetti tried it and was able to play, which prompted a question: Smooth or crunchy?

"Smooth," he said. "Peter Pan."

When the story reached the papers, a local supermarket chain sent about "10 cases" of peanut butter to the Penguins.

"All the guys took them home to their kids," Taglianetti said.

ROLE PLAYERS

It takes a village to raise a Stanley Cup, which is to say, the Penguins needed everyone on their roster to win championships in 1991 and '92.

There was the so-called Muskegon Line—emergency-recall minor leaguers Jock Callander, Mike Needham, and Dave Michayluk from Muskegon of the International League—and players such as Troy Loney, Frank Pietrangelo, Gordie Roberts, Jiri Hrdina, Jim Paek, Jay Caufield, and Randy Gilhen.

Gilhen scored a huge goal with 4:35 left in regulation of Game 2 of a 1991 second-round series against Washington. It tied the score 6-6, and the Penguins won in overtime.

Afterward, nobody could figure out why Gilhen, a 15-goal scorer, had jumped onto the ice on a delayed penalty with the goalie headed to the bench.

Shouldn't one of the stars have gone?

"Nobody jumped, so I did," Gilhen recalled, laughing. "I went right down the ice, the puck came right to me, and I scored.

"The next day, Badger says to me, 'That was a great goal, but if there's ever a delayed penalty again, I don't want you jumping.'"

CRAZY SKATES

No player was as finicky about his equipment as defenseman Paul Coffey. None wore tighter skates, either.

Coffey, perhaps the smoothest skating defenseman in NHL history, had a shoe size of 9 but wore size 6 skates.

"We had the same shoe size, and I'd put his skates on," equipment manager Steve Latin said. "They used to kill my feet. I couldn't imagine going a whole game like that."

Latin also sharpened Coffey's skates flatter than a tabletop because Coffey didn't do the stopping thing.

"He was always on top of the ice, never sunk in," Latin said. "He just wheeled wherever."

Coffey wheeled his way to more points than any defenseman in Penguins history. He rolled up 440 points in 331 regular-season games and tacked on 26 more in 22 playoff games.

BOLD PREDICTION

The sweat on players' faces hadn't yet dried after Game 2 of the 1991 Stanley Cup semifinals at Boston Garden when Penguins left winger Kevin Stevens made a Joe Namath-like guarantee.

Even though the Penguins trailed, two games to none, and even though the Bruins had been to the Cup final the year before, Stevens guaranteed his team would come back and win the best-of-seven series.

He guaranteed it several times, to anyone within earshot.

"We're like, 'What are you doing? You're throwing fuel on the fire,'" teammate Joe Mullen recalled. "Kevin, being Kevin, was like, 'Don't worry about it.'"

Stevens, a Boston native, was ticked off because the Penguins had dominated the game.

"It was one of those heat-of-the-moment, stupid things I used to say, but I just knew we would beat them," he said. "You just believe in guys."

The Penguins were peeved because Boston scored on a five on three with 3:11 left to tie it, then won on Vladimir Ruzicka's over-time goal.

"I felt we deserved better," Stevens said. "So I said what I said, and people ran with it. The guys got a kick out of it . . . and it's always nice when it works out."

The Penguins stormed back to win four straight games. After the season, Boston tried to sign Stevens.

"[The guarantee] got me an offer sheet," Stevens said. "[Bruins GM Mike] Milbury thought it was the best thing that ever happened."

HULK HOGAN

Things got ugly in a 1991 Stanley Cup semifinal, when defenseman Ulf Samuelsson knocked Bruins star Cam Neely out of Game 3 with a second-period check.

The next day, Bruins coach Mike Milbury ripped into Penguins coach "Badger" Bob Johnson.

"For all of Bob Johnson's seven-point plans," Milbury said, "there must have been somewhere in that seven-point plan: 'Make sure you take as many cheap shots as you can against the other team's key players.' So the professor of hockey, as he so often projects himself, is also subtly a professor of goonism, and we can't take that any longer."

Johnson's response to Milbury's tirade: "It's confusing, but it's interesting."

Penguins strength and conditioning coach John Welday—a former offensive tackle at Penn State—had a more pointed response.

At the next day's morning skate at the Civic Arena, Welday donned hockey pads and skates. He added a yellow Hulk Hogan tank top, a Hogan head band and boxing gloves and skated onto the ice with a stick in his hands.

You want a goon? You've got one.

Players and reporters howled. Milbury, sitting at the other end of the arena, looked to see what the commotion was about. He then put a newspaper in front of his face and pretended not to notice.

ODD COUPLE

It was an odd pairing, to be sure. Bryan Trottier, a veteran winding down his NHL career, roomed with long-haired, 18-year-old Czech rookie Jaromir Jagr early in the 1990-91 season.

"His English was bad, and my Czechoslovakian was brutal," Trottier said. "All he watched was MTV. He loved Motley Crew and all that. I loved Country Western."

Still, the two formed a bond and wound up playing with Troy Loney on an effective third line.

"We got really, really close," Trottier said.

KEY ASSIST

Mario Lemieux's back was so bad during the Penguins' Stanley Cup drive in 1991 that he could not tie his skates.

Lemieux had to sit out Game 3 of the final in Minnesota. Before Game 4, he approached locker-room attendant Tracy Luppe with an unusual request.

"He's like, 'Hey, you have to tie my skates,'" Luppe recalled. "I was like, 'You're the best player in the world; how will I be able to tie your skates?' I said, 'All right, and if you don't like them, I'll re-do 'em.'

"He said, 'Yeah, that's the way it's going to have to be.'"

Despite crippling back pain, Mario Lemieux managed to score goals like this against Jon Casey in the '91 Stanley Cup Finals. *(Photo courtesy of the Pittsburgh Penguins)*

Luppe laced Lemieux's skates before each game and between each period.

"He could barely move," Luppe said.

Lemieux still won the Conn Smythe Trophy as playoff MVP and managed to score a few spectacular goals.

"I guess I helped out a little bit," Luppe said. "It's my claim to fame, you could say."

Luppe continued to tie Lemieux's skates at the start of the 1991-92 season and again after Lemieux's dramatic comeback from retirement in 2000.

ELECTRIC ATMOSPHERE

"Badger" Bob Johnson called equipment manager Steve Latin into the coaches room before Game 6 of the 1991 Stanley Cup Final at the Met Center in Minneapolis.

The Penguins led the series, three games to two, and were poised to win the first Stanley Cup in their largely calamitous, 24-year history.

Johnson rubbed his face like always and said, "Well, big guy, whaddaya think?"

Replied Latin: "Badger, you could turn the lights off in that dressing room and they'd go right back on, there's so much electricity in there."

Players could not sit still. They'd start to tie their skates and get up to walk around. Kevin Stevens wouldn't stop talking (not that this was anything new).

Mario Lemieux sat in a corner and said nothing.

"It's a pretty good feeling when you're in a locker room and you know you're not going to lose," Stevens said years later. "Every guy had a job to do, and every guy did it. It's fun when you get everybody on the same page. It doesn't happen that often.

"I'll tell you, I miss it. I wish I could go back there."

Ulf Samuelsson opened the scoring, and the Penguins stormed to a 6-0 lead after two periods.

During the second intermission, Latin recalled, some players cried. Latin, as usual, went to notify Johnson that the third period would start in five minutes.

"He was a wreck," Latin said.

Stevens remembered players trying to stay calm. "Even [goalie] Tommy [Barrasso], who said something once in a blue moon, said something. It was pandemonium, then it got quiet, and everybody realized what was going on. It was 6-0. What do you say?"

Only Johnson could find the right words. He picked up a roll of tape and nervously whacked it against a table in the middle of the dressing room, then delivered the expected instructions for the third period—dump the puck, forecheck, don't give up odd-man breaks, etc.

Johnson rarely swore, but before he left the room, he turned to his players and said, "Men, just remember one thing: In 20 minutes, we're going to be world champions. Don't [screw] it up."

Players fought to get through the door. They scored two more goals in the third period en route to an 8-0 victory.

"Nobody would have thought we'd win a Cup," Lemieux said. "But with Bob Johnson, anything's possible."

LONG, STRANGE TRIP

If the Penguins expected to travel home in luxury the night they won the 1991 Stanley Cup, they were sadly mistaken.

Oh, the flight from Minneapolis to Pittsburgh was fine, but everything that happened thereafter could be filed under the heading, "Comedy of Errors."

The club's travel coordinators were not prepared for the 20,000 fans who crammed the airport and surrounded the team buses—which happened to be school buses on account of a planning glitch.

The players wanted only to get to their cars, but the buses couldn't move amid all the people.

Finally, the bus with the Cup aboard took an alternate route simply to escape the airport. Marketing director Tinsy Labrie was on that bus, along with the likes of Mario Lemieux, Tom Barrasso, Paul Coffey, and Scotty Bowman.

"I remember Tommy Barrasso finally said, 'Let's go to my house and wait it out,'" Labrie said. "So, there we were, sitting on Tom Barrasso's lawn with the Cup on its side as it started to get light out.'"

It would get more surreal. A few members of the group decided to re-board the bus and head back to the airport to pick up their cars.

The bus ran out of gas on a bridge. Members of the Stanley Cup-winning Pittsburgh Penguins were thus relegated to hitchhiking as the sun rose.

"Could this get any more ridiculous?" Labrie wondered.

Soon after, two men on their way to play golf drove by in a pickup truck and asked if the group needed help. The two men recognized a few of the players.

"They were like, 'Do you want a ride?'" Labrie said. "We took it. I wonder if they still tell that story."

Labrie went into the office that morning to plan for a team celebration in downtown Pittsburgh. One of the first co-workers she saw was Chase Edmondson.

"Chase," she said, "We may be Stanley Cup champions, but we're still the Penguins."

• • •

Broadcaster Mike Lange was in one of the two school buses that carried Penguins personnel after their Stanley Cup victory. The bus had two police escorts—one in front and one behind—followed by legions of cars filled with fans.

Things were moving rather slowly, even as the party aboard progressed rapidly. At one point, Lange remembered, a woman yelled at the driver to stop. She ran off the bus and up a hill to relieve herself in the woods.

"Next thing you know, about 25 guys get off the bus and do the same thing—only we didn't go all the way to the woods," Lange said. "We're all standing there, in a row, with about a thousand cars waiting."

CUP FOLLIES

Phil Bourque decided that Mario Lemieux's pool party wasn't lively enough. The Penguins had won the 1991 Stanley Cup a few days earlier, and Lemieux's pool, it should be noted, featured a waterfall lit with neon lights.

"I was sitting in the hot tub with the wives and girlfriends and I go, 'You know what? It's time to get this party started,'" Bourque recalled. "I hiked up the waterfall in my underwear and put the Cup over my head, like King Kong on top of the Empire State Building.

"No disrespect to the Cup or anything, but I heaved it into the swimming pool. There are a whole bunch of pictures out there of it actually in mid-air."

"It wasn't a great idea," said teammate Bob Errey.

The Cup, of course, is hollow. It immediately filled with water and sunk to the bottom of the pool. Bourque dived to retrieve it but had to come up and ask for help.

"It took about four of us to bring the thing up," he said. "But as soon as it went down there, everybody started jumping in the pool, and that's when the party got hopping."

The real party occurred the next day in downtown Pittsburgh, where it seemed as if the entire city came out to celebrate the Penguins' first title.

And if the players were in bad shape that morning, they had nothing on the Cup.

"I understand they needed a silversmith to polish it up that morning, because all the chlorine had tarnished it," Bourque said. "It was kind of a rust brown color."

Worse, the top of the Cup was loose. That is why pictures of that day's celebration show players holding it from the bottom and sides in front of 40,000 fans at Point State Park.

"The bowl was loose, and there was a sign inside the bowl," Errey said. "It said, 'Don't Grab Top of Cup.'"

ROSE GARDEN

On June 24, 1991, the Stanley Cup-champion Penguins became the first NHL team to visit the White House, where president George Bush greeted them.

Thrilled to be there, the players were not insulted when the President said, "And you are?" as Mario Lemieux stepped forward.

"He wasn't a hockey fan," defenseman Larry Murphy said, "and I don't think he was trying to pass himself off as one."

TRAGIC NEWS

As the Penguins celebrated on a bus ride back from the airport after winning their first Stanley Cup, one man was uncharacteristically quiet.

"I remember Badger Bob just sat in the front of the bus," broadcaster Mike Lange said. "He was just not himself."

Johnson, as it turned out, was gravely ill.

Three months later, on August 29, 1991, Martha Johnson had her husband taken to Pittsburgh's Mercy Hospital with stroke-like symptoms. Emergency surgery was performed to remove a tumor, but an inoperable one remained.

"Badger" Bob Johnson had brain cancer. It progressed quickly. He died on November 26, squeezing every last minute out of his life. At the depth of his illness, he was helping his Team USA squad to a silver-medal finish at the Canada Cup by mapping out strategy from his hospital bed.

The Penguins visited Johnson during a preseason trip to Denver. Unable to speak, he wore a Penguins T-shirt and wrote notes to his players.

"We all had an opportunity to look in his eyes for the last time," center Bryan Trottier recalled. "He was such a big part of our success, a big part of the change in the atmosphere of the Penguins organization. His favorite saying said it all: 'It's a great day for hockey.'"

• • •

The night after Johnson's death, Penguins fans paid tribute to him before a Thanksgiving Eve game against New Jersey.

Fans were given battery-powered candles, the Civic Arena ice was inscribed with a message that read, "It's A Great Day For Hockey—Badger Bob," and the arena was darkened as Karla Bonoff sang "Goodbye, My Friend."

"I'll always remember that night, with the lights out and the candles lit," winger Joe Mullen said. "I knew hockey was going to miss Badger very much."

The Penguins scored four of the night's final five goals to win handily. Six days later, coaches, players, wives, and front-office workers flew to Colorado Springs, on the team's way to Edmonton, for Badger Bob's funeral.

Equipment manager Steve Latin keeps one of Johnson's ever-present notebooks, in which Johnson would scribble endlessly.

"I'll open it up when times are rough," Latin said. "When we had that 18-game winless streak [midway through the 2003-04 season], I opened it up and felt better right away."

Considering the impact Johnson had, it's amazing Pittsburgh knew him for only 17 months.

TOCCHET TRADE

In February of 1992, general manager Craig Patrick was set to make his second blockbuster trade in as many years. He was hoping it would propel the Penguins to a Stanley Cup, the way his deal with the Hartford Whalers had the year before.

This time, Patrick wanted to send popular winger Mark Recchi to the Philadelphia Flyers as part of a package that would reel in power forward Rick Tocchet, hulking defenseman Kjell Samuelsson, and veteran goalie Ken Wregget.

Patrick called a meeting that included coach Scotty Bowman and assistant coaches Barry Smith, Rick Kehoe, and Pierre McGuire. He asked everyone to vote on the deal.

Bowman was the only one who voted against it, afraid Recchi would outdo Tocchet.

Penguins fans and players kept "Badger Bob" close to their hearts during the second Stanley Cup run. *(Photo courtesy of the Pittsburgh Penguins)*

Patrick made the trade anyway, and Bowman soon realized that Tocchet provided an element of toughness the Penguins needed, not to mention an excellent scoring touch.

Both were displayed on March 15 at Chicago, shortly after the trade, when Tocchet scored two third-period goals wearing a football-style helmet. He'd left the game in the second period because of a broken jaw.

The Penguins would meet the Blackhawks again in the Stanley Cup final.

"Scotty became a huge Rick Tocchet fan," McGuire recalled. "He realized we needed Tocchet if we were going to beat Chicago in Chicago in the finals."

CLOSED-DOOR MEETING

Eddie Johnston, then Hartford Whalers general manager, was supposed to be the Penguins coach for the 1992-93 season, but the teams could not work out a salary agreement, so Scotty Bowman was retained.

Bowman's return was announced the morning of the team's October 6 opener against Philadelphia and did not produce cheers in the dressing room.

Players weren't thrilled with the way Bowman ran practices (something he didn't do in the final part of his two-year tenure with the Penguins). They would half-jokingly ask equipment manager Steve Latin to hide Bowman's skates and once stuffed cotton in the airhorn Bowman used to signal line changes.

Late in Bowman's first season behind the bench—1991-92—the issue came to a head during a meeting March 2 at the team hotel in Calgary.

There were no coaches present, just general manager Craig Patrick and the players. Patrick called the gathering. The team had won only two of its previous 12 games and was threatening to become the first Stanley Cup champion in 22 years to miss the playoffs.

Everybody sat in a small ballroom.

"Our team was just in disarray," winger Phil Bourque recalled.

After a few players spouted clichés about working harder and the like, Bourque, Peter Taglianetti, and Bob Errey, among others, spoke up.

"I flat-out said to Craig, 'I don't think we can win with Scotty Bowman,'" Bourque recalled. "Everybody kind of scooched back in their seats like holy [cow], what the heck is he doing?"

Patrick did not say much. He sat and listened as other players chimed in with their thoughts.

According to Bourque, Patrick said, "Scotty is very different, but he is the winningest coach in hockey, and there's a reason why. Maybe you don't understand it now. I agree with everything everybody's saying, except for what [Bourque] said. I think we can win with Scotty Bowman, and we will win with Scotty Bowman."

Patrick subsequently spoke with Bowman, and the situation improved.

"We each took a step toward each other," Bourque said. "From there, it was a different hockey team."

STRANGE LINE

Nobody could believe it when Scotty Bowman wrote out his lines on the chalkboard before Game 1 of a 1992 playoff series against the Washington Capitals.

Mario Lemieux was injured, so Bowman put checker Troy Loney between high scorers Kevin Stevens and Rick Tocchet.

"Everybody was kind of looking at me, and I was like, 'What?'" Loney said. "Scotty never asked me if I'd played center before—which I hadn't—he just threw me in there, which was typical of the way he could keep you off balance.

"Well, I think Tocchet and Stevens were sour as hell, but I was having a great time."

The experiment lasted approximately 10 minutes.

GRAVES ATTACK

New York Rangers forward Adam Graves became a marked man in Pittsburgh during a 1992 playoff series, when his wicked, base-ball-swing slash broke Mario Lemeiux's left hand at 5:05 of the second period of Game 2.

Lemieux was finished for the series and was not expected back in the playoffs. The NHL suspended Graves for four games, but only after he scored in a 6-5 victory in Game 3 that gave the Rangers a 2-1 lead in the best-of-seven series.

Graves' comment: "Obviously, you have to be more cautious in the way you're checking a guy."

Lemieux ripped the NHL as "too dangerous" and said he felt the Roger Neilson-led Rangers had put out "a contract" on him.

The incident sparked the Penguins, who roared back from a 4-2 deficit midway through the third period to win Game 4, 6-5 in over-time.

Ron Francis started the rally when he beat Mike Richter from behind the blue line, just after a five-minute major against the Pen-guins had expired.

"I was just looking to get off the ice," Francis recalled.

The shot caromed in off Richter's glove.

"You can't give them an inch," Richter told reporters. "But that's what I gave them: an inch."

The Penguins took a mile. Jaromir Jagr stole Game 5 with a spec-tacular performance, including a penalty-shot goal.

Lemieux returned in the following series against Boston with a small cast on his left hand. In order to allow him to grip his sticks, the training staff shaved the tops of them as thin as a putter.

• • •

Enigmatic coach Scotty Bowman sends Bob Errey over the boards in 1991-92. *(Photo courtesy of the Pittsburgh Penguins)*

When Francis arrived home after scoring a hat trick in Game 4, he found a few hats hanging from a small tree in his yard. His next-door neighbor had put them there.

"The next morning, there had to be about 25 hats on that tree," Francis said. "It was pretty funny."

PIECE OF ART

Mario Lemieux put the perfect finishing touch on the Penguins' playoff sweep of the Boston Bruins in 1992.

The Penguins were short-handed late in Game 4, leading 4-1, when Lemieux knocked the puck out of mid-air and headed down the ice against future Hall of Fame defenseman Raymond Bourque. Penguins players stood on the bench to watch what would become one of the great goals in team annals.

Lemieux tortured Bourque, throwing the puck at his feet so that Bourque could not turn around.

Finally, Lemieux grabbed the puck with a dramatic swoop and roofed a shot over goaltender Andy Moog's left shoulder from about two feet out.

"It was an amazing thing," said Penguins winger Kevin Stevens.

Bruins coach Rick Bowness called the goal "a piece of art."

Bourque, of course, was the same man Lemieux had victimized on his first NHL goal, eight years earlier.

SETTING A TRAP

The Penguins of the early 1990s are remembered as a free-wheeling, offensive juggernaut, but they wouldn't have won their second Stanley Cup if they hadn't dropped into a passive, 1-4 trap against the Washington Capitals in a second-round series.

Washington had built a three-games-to-one lead by capitalizing on Penguins turnovers and by springing their active and talented defense into the rush.

Basically, the Capitals were waiting for the overaggressive Penguins to mess up.

A day before Game 5, the Penguins decided they could play the waiting game, too. Mario Lemieux and Ron Francis approached coach Scotty Bowman with the idea of playing a 1-4 system that would clog the neutral zone.

"I was in the training room," recalled forward Bryan Trottier. "Mario and Ronnie were talking about how Washington was counteracting our forecheck. They said we could clog everything at the blue line, not be as aggressive and go into a 1-4. In our end, if the Capitals dumped it in, [goaltender] Tommy [Barrasso] could play the puck so well, he could just fire it out on his forehand.

"I don't remember Scotty being all that enthusiastic about it, but when you're down 1-3, you're willing to give it a shot."

The strategy achieved swift and stunning results.

"It changed the series right around," winger Joe Mullen said.

The Penguins grabbed a 3-0 lead in Game 5 and won the final three games by a combined score of 14-7.

THE SLIDE

It was softspoken general manager Craig Patrick, of all people, who sparked a chain of events that led to Bryan Trottier's memorable slide at a 1992 Stanley Cup celebration.

The 40,000 fans who filled Three Rivers Stadium that day were growing a bit restless in the drizzle.

"We were waiting for the mayor or something," Trottier said. "Well, Craig comes up to me and goes, 'We better do something to get the crowd going. Grab the Cup and do something.'"

Trottier asked a group of teammates to join him in a romp around the stadium. They agreed but left him out to dry when he stepped off the podium.

"I took four steps away, and all those guys were grinning, those creeps," Trottier said. "Now, I'm feeling a little conspicuous. At the same time, I said, 'I'm committed.'"

Adam Graves became enemy No. 1 in Pittsburgh when he broke Mario Lemieux's wrist with a wicked slash in the '92 playoffs. *(Photo by James M. Kubus/Pittsburgh Tribune-Review)*

Trottier saw that the infield tarp looked mighty slick. Without a second thought, he took a running start and slid on his back, the Cup clenched in his hands.

The splashy slide seemed as if it would never end. The crowd went wild.

"Craig slapped me on the back and said, 'That was great,'" Trottier said. "It turned out to be something a lot of people remember. I'll bump into people at airports, malls, wherever, and they say, 'That was awesome.'"

STANLEY HEADS TO THE HOSPITAL

The Penguins arrived home from Chicago in the wee hours of the morning after winning their second straight Stanley Cup in 1992. The equipment men and trainers were showering when locker-room attendant Tracy Luppe announced he was going to take the Cup for a little spin.

Luppe's girlfriend worked at West Penn Hospital, so he loaded the Cup onto the back of his truck and drove it there for a visit.

It had only been 10 hours since the end of the game.

"I stunk like champagne and everything, and when I got on the elevator at the hospital, everybody was like, 'Oh my God, that's the Stanley Cup,'" Luppe recalled.

He walked into the labor and delivery department, where his girlfriend worked, and said, "Here's the Stanley Cup. I need some sleep."

Luppe grabbed a power nap in a delivery room, while the rest of the floor went nuts. Newborns were photographed in the Cup. Adults were photographed next to it.

"No way was anybody getting any help at the time," Luppe said. "When I woke up, you couldn't move, there were so many people on the floor."

LIFE'S A BEACH

Jaromir Jagr made quite a stir in Pittsburgh after delivering a memorable quote to *Sports Illustrated* in the summer of 1992. The team had just won its second consecutive Stanley Cup, but money problems were rearing their ugly head. The Penguins had a long history of such problems.

The future held a few, as well.

"If they have no money, I want to be traded where there's beaches," Jagr said. "I have two Stanley Cup rings. I don't need more rings. I just need money and beaches and girls."

Jagr never did get another ring. He was traded in the summer of 2001.

GARAGE LEAGUE

On January 26, 1992, Mario Lemieux tore into the NHL after a 6-4 loss at Washington, in which the Capitals had basically mugged the faster, more talented Penguins.

Jaromir Jagr was so frustrated that he knocked referee Ron Hoggarth to his knees during the game.

Afterward, Lemieux fired off a memorable scolding.

"It's a skating and passing game—that's what the fans want to see," he said. "The advantage is to the marginal player now. That's the way this garage league is run."

Commissioner John Ziegler fined Lemieux $1,000.

MIRACLE MAN

Philadelphia sports fans once booed Santa Claus, but they couldn't help but cheer Mario Lemieux on March 2, 1993, when he performed perhaps the most dramatic feat of his career.

Fewer than 12 hours before the puck dropped, Lemieux was undergoing the last of his radiation treatments for Hodgkin's disease.

Soon after, he boarded a plane to Philadelphia. Fans gave him a 90-second ovation when he appeared on the ice for the national anthem.

Coach Scotty Bowman planned to play Lemieux limited minutes, but that went out the window in the first period.

"We didn't think he was ready yet, but that's Mario," winger Joe Mullen said. "He played a great game that night, too."

Lemieux finished with a goal and an assist in a 5-4 loss.

"I wanted to come back earlier," he told reporters. "But the doctors wouldn't let me."

• • •

When he returned from his treatments for Hodgkin's disease, Lemieux trailed Buffalo's Pat LaFontaine by 12 points in the NHL

Bryan Trottier takes his memorable slide on the rain-covered tarp at Three Rivers Stadium. *(Photo courtesy of the Pittsburgh Penguins)*

scoring race. The deficit shrank quickly. Lemieux racked up 30 goals and 56 points in the final 20 games to finish with 160 points. He won the scoring title by 12 points.

"I thought about it even during radiation," Lemieux said. "I was determined to come back and regain the lead."

UGLY INCIDENT

Former television analyst Paul Steigerwald recalled a horrific night in 1993, when play-by-play man Mike Lange was attacked on the street in Toronto.

"I had just returned to the hotel from the morning skate, when Mike called and asked me to come to his room. I knocked on the door, and he stood behind it as he invited me in," Steigerwald said. "When I stepped into the room, I was horrified by the sight of this almost unrecognizable apparition. His face was literally four times its normal size, and his lips were the size of hot dogs. I am not exaggerating when I say he looked an awful lot like the 'Elephant Man.'"

Lange proceeded to tell his partner what happened the night before. Some nutcase apparently ran up and sucker-punched Lange in the jaw as Lange munched a slice of pizza. He spent most of the night in the hospital having his teeth repaired.

Steigerwald thought Lange was going to ask him to handle the play-by-play that night, but Lange explained that he wanted Steigerwald to be on camera by myself to open the telecast, then toss it to Lange off-camera for the faceoff.

Jaromir Jagr and Mario Lemieux celebrate their second consecutive Stanley Cup victory. (Photo courtesy of the Pittsburgh Penguins)

"His speech was slightly garbled, and he spoke rather economically, but he was otherwise on top of his game," Steigerwald said. "It has to be considered one the most incredible performances in the history of sports broadcasting—and it was typical of Mike's unflappable belief that the show must go on. It should not surprise you to know that he never has missed a broadcast because of illness in all his years with the Penguins."

AT WHAT COST?

Most would agree that the 1992-93 Penguins, with four 100-point scorers, were the best team in franchise history.

"By far," left winger Kevin Stevens said. "We were a machine."

Certainly, they were heavy favorites to win a third consecutive Stanley Cup after finishing the season with an NHL-record 17-game winning streak (and a tie in the season finale).

The Penguins knew they were on a roll when defenseman Ulf Samuelsson—who had 11 goals in 277 games with the team—beat Montreal's Patrick Roy in overtime on April 7, giving the team its 15th consecutive victory. That tied the New York Islanders' league record.

But the winning streak, as it turned out, might have spent valuable energy reserves that would have come in handy in a second-round playoff series against—who else?—the Islanders.

Players such as Ron Francis have said the team became consumed with the streak, to the point where it might have been a distraction, or perhaps bred overconfidence.

"We were winning; the problem was, we weren't playing well," defenseman Larry Murphy said. "We were just kind of fluking our way through the whole thing. Once we got into the playoffs, we didn't handle adversity too well."

The Islanders eliminated the Penguins in seven games. Stevens doesn't believe the streak affected his team negatively.

"The Islanders always gave us fits," he said. "We had one tough series every year, and it was going to be that series that year. We had to find a way to get by them, and we didn't. We could've beaten the rest of those teams skating backwards."

HORRIFIC INJURY

Kevin Stevens wanted to hit New York Islanders defenseman Rich Pilon something fierce. It was early in the first period of the seventh game of a second-round playoff series in 1993.

"He was playing on me the whole series, driving me crazy," Stevens recalled. "We had 10 years of history, too. I just went to hit him, and I really hit him. But he had his shield on, and he leads with his head, and I got knocked out."

In mid-air, no less.

Stevens landed face-first with a sickening thud. He sustained a broken nose and a fractured frontal sinus bone. The injury required several hours of reconstructive surgery.

The way Stevens sees it, the Penguins might have avoided a stunning 4-3 loss to the underdog Islanders if not for the incident.

"I think I could have made a difference somewhere in there."

CRUSHING BLOW

The name David Volek is enough to turn stomachs all over Pittsburgh.

Volek's goal at 5:16 of overtime in Game 7 of a 1993 second-round playoff series stunned a Civic Arena crowd and gave the upstart New York Islanders a 4-3 victory.

The best team in Penguins history was finished. A potential dynasty was ruined.

This was the third time the Islanders eliminated the Penguins in the deciding game of a playoff series.

A rugged young defenseman named Darius Kasparaitis—who would later join the Penguins—tortured Jaromir Jagr and Mario Lemieux, and Islanders coach Al Arbour made all the right moves.

"It was one of Al's greatest coaching jobs, shuffling lines and matching personnel," said former Islanders GM Bill Torrey.

The Islanders played the series without their best player, Pierre Turgeon.

"Without a doubt, we should have won it," said Penguins defenseman Larry Murphy. "It just goes to show: The best team doesn't always win the Stanley Cup."

Lemieux would later say that he'd run out of gas by playoff time. Understandably so, considering he spent part of the season battling Hodgkin's disease.

Kevin Stevens was a powerful force in both of the Penguins' Stanley Cup seasons. *(Photo courtesy of the Pittsburgh Penguins)*

MARATHON GAME

As much as the Islanders tormented the Penguins, so the Penguins tormented the Washington Capitals.

Never more so than on April 24, 1996, at USAir Arena, when the Penguins won Game 4 of a first-round playoff series, 3-2, at precisely 79:15 of overtime.

In other words, the teams played a doubleheader and then some. It was the third longest game in NHL history and the longest in six decades.

Petr Nedved's winning goal occurred six hours, 37 minutes after the opening faceoff, as Mario Lemieux and Tom Barrasso watched on television.

Barrasso left the game with back spasms at the start of the second period. Lemieux had been tossed out in the second period for attacking Todd Krygier, who had dumped Lemieux to the ice without a penalty (Lemieux later joked that he should be able to rejoin the action, seeing as he'd sat out the equivalent of a full game).

Among the other sidelights:

- Penguins coach Eddie Johnston was hit by a puck on the bench, opening a gash on his head that required 18 stitches to close.
- Penguins goalie Ken Wregget stopped the first overtime penalty shot in playoff history (Joe Juneau) and made 53 saves.
- Capitals rookie Olaf Kolzig made 62 saves.
- Fans without tickets showed up at the rink during the overtimes, walked in for free and watched.

Nedved finally won it on the power play with 44.6 seconds left in the fourth overtime. He took a pass from Sergei Zubov and fired a turnaround wrist shot from the left circle that sailed through a crowd and over Kolzig's left shoulder.

"It was getting to the point," Nedved said, "where I didn't really think anybody was going to score."

WEIGHT OF THE WORLD

Mario Lemieux's wife, Nathalie, endured a difficult pregnancy with the couple's first son. It kept her husband on edge for weeks, although his struggle was only known among the Penguins' inner circle.

When Austin Lemieux finally arrived in a premature birth, his father was highly relieved—and greatly inspired.

He was ready to play hockey again. The St. Louis Blues were next on the schedule, and it just happened to be Wayne Gretzky's first (and last) game in Pittsburgh as a member of the St. Louis Blues.

March 26, 1996.

Lemieux ranks the game among his best hockey memories. He finished with five goals and eight points in an 8-4 victory. It tied the single-best performance of his career.

On his final goal of the night, Lemieux took a pass from Ron Francis, beat goalie Jon Casey and finally came to rest on his back against the end boards, where he lay on the ice with a giddy smile—as if he had amazed even himself.

ONE-PUNCH KNOCKOUT

Maybe it was the boxing lessons Chris Tamer took as a teen. Whatever the case, he delivered one of the more dramatic punches in Penguins history when he felled Chicago Blackhawks heavyweight Bob Probert with a short left during Tamer's rookie season in 1996.

Tamer never became a noted NHL fighter, but that punch gave him a lasting reputation.

"I guess he didn't see that left coming," Tamer later said. "He was facing my left side and obviously didn't have a tight grip on it. I don't get a great deal of satisfaction from that. I give myself credit for just showing up for the fight."

FAREWELL, MARIO

Few expected the Penguins to win the Stanley Cup in 1997. They'd blown a golden chance the year before, losing to the underdog Florida Panthers in the Eastern Conference final.

To add to the gloom, Mario Lemieux left little doubt that the 1996-97 season would be his last. He confirmed as much in early April, and it seemed as if he would go out quietly.

The Penguins trailed the Philadelphia Flyers in a first-round series, three games to none, going into Game 4 at the Civic Arena.

Mustering some untapped heart, the Penguins jumped on the Flyers early and were ahead 3-1 as the clock started to wind down.

Fans began chanting Lemieux's name—"Mar-ee-oh! Mar-ee-oh!"—midway through the third period. Everyone realized this

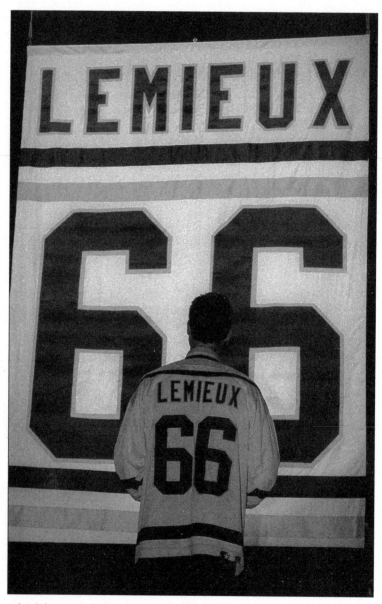

Little did anyone know that when Mario Lemieux's jersey was raised to the rafters in 1997, it would be lowered three years later. *(Photo by James M. Kubus/Pittsburgh Tribune-Review)*

could be his last game in Pittsburgh, because the series was shifting to Philadelphia for Game 5.

Could Le Magnifique possibly produce one last piece of drama? Of course he could.

With 1:04 left, he took a pass from Ian Moran and skated in on a breakaway against goalie Garth Snow. The building seemed to hold its breath.

It exploded in cheers when Lemieux scored a picture-perfect goal. He promptly looked to the heavens with his hands outstretched, palms up, as if to offer thanks.

"It was perfect," said the Penguins' Craig Patrick, who was interim coach at the time. "Couldn't write a better script than that."

The normally stoic Lemieux, just 31 at the time, played the final seconds with tears welling in his eyes (the Penguins lost the next game).

"It's the first time I've cried after a game," he said. "It's something I'll always remember."

The rest of Pittsburgh cried with him, realizing that one of the great athletes of the 20th century was never to perform in front of them again.

Or so they thought.

5

HIGHS AND LOWS

(1997–2004)

WHAT A DRAG

Star right winger Jaromir Jagr got himself into plenty of hot water in the summer of 1999, when the Czech tabloid *Blesk* ran a story in which he was quoted as saying the difference between his native Czech Republic and Pittsburgh was like the difference "between heaven and hell."

Jagr insisted he'd been misquoted, just as he had a few months earlier when a Czech newspaper quoted him ripping Penguins coach Kevin Constantine.

It just so happened that when the *Blesk* story came out, Jagr was photographed dressed in drag for a charity function in the Czech Republic. He wore a red wig, blush and lipstick to go with a flowery dress.

The *Hockey News* ran both stories with a brilliant headline: "Miss Quote."

JAYWALKER

A simple search for a dinner spot turned into a fiasco one night in Calgary when long-haired, Lithuanian defenseman Darius Kasparaitis was cited for jaywalking.

Kasparaitis was ordered into the back of a squad car. He refused. He waited for teammates Brad Werenka, Hans Jonsson, and Rob Brown to catch up.

After the players piled into the back seat, Kasparaitis proceeded to tell the officer that Werenka was from Mexico. The officer threat-

Jaromir Jagr as "Miss Quote." *(Photo by Ales Krecl/AFP)*

ened to kick Kasparaitis out of the country, which would have put a crimp in his plans to play the following night.

"The cop started getting a sense of humor after talking to Kaspar for about 15 minutes," Werenka said. "He lightened up and drove us to a restaurant."

Eventually, Kasparaitis offered the cop tickets to the next night's game. Brown recalled that by the end of the ride, the players were laughing so hard they were crying.

"Only Kaspar could cause these kinds of problems," Brown said. "He could have been the first Lithuanian kicked out of Canada."

WANNA FIGHT?

When a 55-year-old Florida Panthers fan named Keith Hubbell made fun of Matthew Barnaby's injured eye, he had no idea Barnaby would take such offense.

Obviously, he didn't know Barnaby very well.

The incident occurred moments after Barnaby held on for dear life in an altercation with towering Panthers enforcer Peter Worrell. As Barnaby left the ice and headed down the runway to the dressing room, Hubbell, seated next to the Penguins' bench, yelled to him, 'How many fingers do I have up?'"

Barnaby turned around and raced toward Hubbell. He reached into the stands and grabbed Hubbell's arm. Hubbell then cocked his fists as if he was ready to fight.

He was glad he didn't.

"You would be talking to a dead man," he said.

Barnaby was suspended for four games, forfeiting $53,658.54 of his $1.1 million salary.

HAIRY SITUATION

Training camp wasn't 10 minutes old in 1999 when word began to spread about the biggest cut in Penguins history.

Jaromir Jagr's hair was gone.

Most of it, anyway. Jagr's trademark curly locks were strewn on a barbershop floor in Rome.

"I was in Italy and told them to make me look like an Italian," Jagr told reporters. "They have short hair like this. . . . I think I'm old enough to have short hair now."

Jagr's teammates were astounded to see that their captain, who once could have passed for a rock star, now looked like a linebacker for the University of Pittsburgh's football team.

"I had to introduce myself to him," teammate Tyler Wright said.

GOAL JUDGE

On September 3, 1999, inside a federal courtroom at the USX Tower in downtown Pittsburgh, US Bankruptcy Judge Bernard J. Markovitz pulled off one of the great plays in Penguins history.

Markovitz weaved through 10 months of red tape and political haggling to set up Mario Lemieux for a tap-in goal.

In authorizing Lemieux's plan to buy the franchise out of bankruptcy, Markovitz likely prevented the NHL from disbanding the team, or perhaps relocating it to a city such as Portland, Oregon.

The Penguins had been $100 million in debt when they filed for bankruptcy the previous October.

Lemieux said goodbye to more than $20 million owed to him on his final contract and took a $25 million equity stake in the team. He defeated Civic Arena operator SMG and Fox Sports Pittsburgh, who banded together in an attempt to outbid him.

The Penguins had spent nearly a year snared in tumultuous bankruptcy proceedings. Markovitz needed less than a half-hour to settle the matter.

The judge looked up from his chair and said, "All right, this is done. Now the puck is on Mr. Lemieux's stick, and we've all seen what he's been able to do with that."

The Penguins broke even in their first four seasons under Lemieux's ownership.

WORLD BEATERS

The Penguins took center stage when the Czech Republic stunned the world by winning an Olympic gold medal in 1998 in Nagano, Japan.

Four Penguins—Jaromir Jagr, Robert Lang, Martin Straka and Jiri Slegr—were key members of the Czech team. They took part in a wild celebration in Prague's Old Town Square, where more than 130,000 adoring fans came to cheer, then boarded a plane for Montreal.

Though bleary-eyed from more than 30 hours of travel over the previous three days, they led the way in a 6-2 victory over the Canadiens.

Lang scored 52 seconds into the game. Jagr had four points.

All four players will forever remember the party in Prague.

"When we came off the plane and I saw all the people, I started crying," Straka said. "My dream came true."

"We were not playing for ourselves," Jagr told the crowd. "We were playing for 10 million people."

HEARD 'ROUND THE LEAGUE

This must have been what the Coliseum in ancient Rome sounded like. Penguins fans cheered maniacally on March 7, 1998, as Philadelphia Flyers star Eric Lindros crawled along the ice, desperately trying to regain his senses.

Seconds earlier, Lindros had absorbed a knockout hit from Penguins defenseman Darius Kasparaitis. The Penguins trailed 4-3 with 11:12 left in the second period. Momentum quickly turned.

Lindros sustained a concussion—one of many that would eventually threaten his career—and stayed overnight at a Pittsburgh hospital.

The Penguins won, 6-4, but the same two teams were scheduled to play the next night in Philadelphia. Kasparaitis might as well have had his face plastered on a most-wanted sign.

A little more than three minutes into the game, Dainius Zubrus and Rod Brind'Amour tried to gang-tackle Kasparaitis. After the Flyers scored a power-play goal, they went after him again.

Brind'Amour drilled him, then Colin Forbes pounded him behind the Penguins' net.

"I knew they were going to come after me," Kasparaitis said, flashing his mischievous smile. "I just had to be careful."

GREAT GOAL

Jaromir Jagr had a knack for scoring dramatic and spectacular goals. Few, if any, were more spectacular than the one he scored on March 13, 1999, in a home game against the Philadelphia Flyers.

Flyers defenseman Luke Richardson pulled Jagr to the ice on the play, but Jagr still managed to release a weak backhander. The puck deflected off goalie Ron Hextall's blocker, and Jagr, sliding on his

Darius Kasparaitis left an indelible mark on Penguins history.
(Photo courtesy of the Pittsburgh Penguins)

stomach, reached up and flicked it under the crossbar for his 32nd goal and 100th point of the season.

"We're witnessing something that's going to be on the highlight reel forever, regarding one of the greatest goals ever scored," Penguins coach Kevin Constantine said.

Jagr called the goal "an accident."

Others knew better.

"Maybe it was lucky," teammate Martin Straka said. "But it's the great players who get lucky all the time."

NOWHERE TO BE FOUND

When the Penguins started 8-14-3 under Kevin Constantine in 1999-2000, general manager Craig Patrick decided it was time for a change.

Constantine had presided over the best defensive team in Penguins history—and the only division winner between 1996-2004—two seasons earlier, but his relationship with Jagr had soured. The team had gone south.

Patrick called on old friend, Herb Brooks, who was scouting for the Penguins. Patrick had been Brooks' assistant coach with the U.S. Olympic team in 1980 and was convinced that Brooks could help turn the team around, if only he could be found.

Brooks, near his home in Minnesota, was getting his transmission fluid changed at the time.

"The guy at the station said, 'Hey, there's a phone call,'" Brooks said. "I said, 'Who in the heck knows I'm here, other than my wife?'"

Brooks had been out of coaching for eight years. He returned intent on allowing his star players to be creative.

That was nothing new. While coaching the New York Rangers, he said of flashy forward Pierre Larouche, "Having Pierre Larouche check is like having Picasso paint a garage."

DOG DAYS

Coach Herb Brooks missed a practice for a very unusual reason one day.

Brooks lived out of a hotel during his six-month tenure as Penguins coach. Goaltender J. S. Aubin lived nearby. One day, Brooks was taking a stroll when he spotted Aubin and his girlfriend walking their dog.

When the Penguins faltered early in the 1999-2000 season, Craig Patrick called on old friend Herb Brooks. *(Photo courtesy of the Pittsburgh Penguins)*

As Brooks reached down to pet the dog, his back went out.

"I said to J. S., 'Your dog jumped on me, pushed me, and my back went out, so it's a lawsuit,'" Brooks said the next day, laughing. "I'm going to call your agent."

HERBIE GOES NUTS

Before Herb Brooks came along, Bob Berry was the Penguins' undisputed champion of coaching tirades.

Brooks snatched the crown on January 13, 2000, when he engaged Colorado Avalanche television broadcasters Peter McNab and John Kelly after a 4-3 loss at Colorado.

The exchange occurred in a corridor at the Pepsi Center, near the Penguins dressing room, roughly 15 minutes after the game.

Brooks had just seen a replay of an unpenalized cross check by Colorado's Alexei Gusarov, who hit Penguins winger Matthew Barnaby in the back of the neck with 27.4 seconds left.

Brooks took exception to the fact that Kelly, son of late and legendary St. Louis Blues play-by-play man Dan Kelly, said, "Barnaby has a tendency to embellish," as Barnaby lay on the ice injured.

After Brooks' brief but animated exchange with McNab, Kelly walked past.

Brooks: "Hey, did you make that call on Barnaby?"

Kelly: "What's that?"

Brooks: "Did you say he has a tendency to embellish, when he's down on the ice? Was that your call?"

Kelly: "Herb, do you want to talk about it?"

Brooks: "Was that your call? Was that your call? Was that your call? Was that your call? You say he has a tendency to embellish? He almost tore his head off; he could have killed him. And you said, 'He has a tendency to embellish.' You've got a long way to go to live up to your father's reputation after a cheap shot like that! Did you get a [expletive] life-long contract here? I can't believe that."

Kelly: "That's my opinion, Herb."

Brooks: "That's your opinion? Well, it's a [double expletive] opinion, you understand? Get your [double expletive] out of here!"

Kelly: "You're not going to kick me out of here."

Brooks: "I'll kick your [butt] all over the place, all right? (Brooks pushed Kelly, and the two were separated by an NHL security man.) Cheap shot. Has a tendency to embellish. I can't believe that, Kelly. I can't believe that. Go look at the tape."

• • •

Two days later in Nashville, Brooks found out the NHL had suspended him two games.

Between the time he learned of the suspension and spotted a reporter on the street, he was approached by a beggar.

"What did you say to him, Herb?" the reporter asked.

"I gave him $5 and said, 'I'm having a little trouble myself today.'"

THE LONGEST GAME

At the end of the fourth overtime, ESPN broadcaster Steve Levy walked over to the writers' section of the press box at Mellon Arena and said, "We're going to be on *ESPN Classic* by the time this is done."

Game 4 of this second-round playoff series, played on May 4, 2000, ended at precisely 12:01 of the fifth overtime, or 2:35 a.m., when Philadelphia's Keith Primeau beat goaltender Ron Tugnutt from the right faceoff circle to give his team a 2-1 victory.

At 152 minutes, one second, it was the third longest NHL game ever played.

Children slept. The press box ran out of beverages. Players took intravenous fluids, changed shirts and pads, and gobbled pizza between periods.

"It's certainly hard to describe a game like this," said Penguins coach Herb Brooks. "Where do you start, and where do you finish?"

Start with this: The Flyers were lucky the game went to overtime.

The Penguins held a 1-0 lead when Martin Straka went to the penalty box at 4:47 of the third period. Four seconds later, Flyers winger John LeClair apparently deflected Eric Desjardins' shot past Tugnutt.

The play went to video review to determine whether LeClair tipped the puck with a high stick. Tugnutt and his teammates were positive he had. Replays were inconclusive.

It was a long time before anyone scored again. Eventually, players were skating on fumes.

"You're not even thinking about what you're doing," said Penguins winger Kovalev. "Your body is playing for you."

Among the more remarkable statistics:

- Jaromir Jagr played 59:08.
- Flyers defenseman Dan McGillis led all players by logging 61:05 of ice time.
- Desjardins took 73 shifts.
- Kovalev had 10 shots on goal and missed the net on 10 other attempts.
- Penguins defenseman Peter Popovic blocked nine shots.
- Tugnutt played more minutes (152:01) and made more saves (70) than any goaltender in Penguins' history.
- Flyers goalie Brian Boucher kept the Penguins scoreless for 149:39 after Kovalev's goal at 2:22 of the first period.

The previous longest game in team history occurred April 24, 1996, at Washington, when Petr Nedved beat the Capitals at 79 minutes, 15 seconds of overtime.

Eddie Johnston was on the bench for both games. In the first, he was the Penguins' head coach. In the second, an assistant.

He left with very different feelings the second time, and so did the Penguins, who now found themselves tied in a series they once led two games to none.

They would not win again.

MAN BEHIND THE SCENES

Long after most people had gone home after the third longest game in NHL history, 80-year-old Anthony "A.T." Caggiano was busily working inside the Penguins dressing room.

The Penguins had lost a five-overtime game to the Philadelphia Flyers. The clock read 3:30 a.m.

It proved to be the last game of A.T.'s incredible career. He died 12 days later, saddening the entire Penguins family. A.T. had been involved with Pittsburgh hockey longer than anyone.

Longer, even, than the Penguins' original general manager, Jack Riley.

A.T. started in the 1950s with the old Pittsburgh Hornets of the American Hockey League, and after games, he could be found fishing pucks out of the nets after warm ups, filling water bottles, or performing any of a variety of tasks.

"You could call anybody on any team and they know who A.T. is," said Penguins locker-room attendant Tracy Luppe, "up to and including 'Gretz' [Wayne Gretzky]."

ROUGH NIGHT

A bunch of weary Penguins returned home from Tokyo in October, 2000, after opening the regular season there with a two-game set against the Nashville Predators.

When time stood still: Keith Primeau's goal finally ended it at 12:01 of the fifth overtime, or 2:35 a.m. (Photo by James M. Kubus/Pittsburgh Tribune-Review)

Not everybody could stay awake when the Pens and Flyers played five overtimes in the 2000 playoffs. *(Photo by James M. Kubus/Pittsburgh Tribune-Review)*

The team traveled 15 hours on a Monday, arriving home at around 6 p.m. It's hard to imagine anyone's first night was rougher—or stranger—than defenseman Ian Moran's.

"I got home, had a bowl of Golden Grahams, a bagel, two puddings, turned on *Monday Night Football* and woke up with drool all down the front of my T-shirt," he said.

Had Moran's wife not been in Boston, she would have had a premier photo opportunity.

Her husband's night wasn't finished.

"I went upstairs, took a shower, trimmed my beard, fell asleep until around one, was wide awake from one until four, fell back asleep at 8:30 and slept unbelievable. Woke up again with one of my dogs in the bed and had no idea where I was and what I was doing."

STUNNING NEWS

In late November of 2000, Penguins executive Tom McMillan arranged for what he thought would be a brief, informal meeting with owner Mario Lemieux, who hadn't been seen around the office in a month.

Lemieux's absence was somewhat unusual but didn't raise many eyebrows.

Strangely, though, he called team president Tom Rooney into the office and put his hand up as McMillan began to talk.

"There's been a little change in plans," Lemieux said. "We're going to be moving in a different direction."

Rooney and McMillan, the team's main marketers, feared the worst. Would Lemieux, who had retired three years earlier, relinquish his ownership?

Lemieux leaned forward and said, "I'm coming back."

McMillan remembered waiting for the punch line.

Rooney leaned toward Lemieux and said, "As a player?"

Lemieux, who had been training for the previous month, laughed and said, "Yeah."

"That's when it hit me—he's serious," McMillan said. "It was a surreal situation. I started thinking, 'Everything just changed. All the stuff we've been working on, rip it up.'"

Many details would need to be worked out, particularly the part about Lemieux, then 35, becoming the first full-time sports owner to suit up and play for his team.

But it's not as if the NHL was going to stand in his way.

LEMIEUX DEBUT, PART II

It hardly looked as if Mario Lemieux had gone more than 1,200 days without a competitive game of hockey.

The hockey world stood at attention on December 27, 2000, when Lemieux—already a member of the Hockey Hall of Fame— made his comeback in a home game against the Toronto Maple Leafs. More than 300 press credentials were issued.

Lemieux seemed like an apparition when he raced to center ice at 7:05 p.m. for warmups. The crowd roared at first, then simply stood and watched, as if they couldn't believe what they were seeing.

They roared again when public address announcer John Barbero said, "Add to the Pittsburgh lineup, No. 66, Mario Lemieux."

The lights went down at 7:37 p.m., and Lemieux's No. 66 banner was lowered from the rafters with his four-year-old son, Austin, watching on the ice. Again, the crowd cheered loudly for a moment, then waited.

In their dressing room, the Penguins waited anxiously to take the ice with their 35-year-old owner-turned-player.

"We all tried to talk, but it was weird," defenseman Darius Kasparaitis said. "I hadn't felt that nervous for many years."

As usual, Lemieux delivered the drama.

Seconds into his first shift, he tried his old bank-the-puck-off-the-goalie trick from behind the net. Jaromir Jagr swooped in for the loose puck and tipped it home at the 33-second mark.

The goal stood after a video review. Lemieux had assist No. 882. He finished with a goal and two assists and the knowledge that his son finally got to see him play in NHL game.

Afterward in the dressing room, Austin Lemieux, then a toddler, walked up to his father and said, "I saw you playing. . . . I saw you."

BLOOD BROTHERS

When Matthew Barnaby was traded from Buffalo to Pittsburgh, everybody asked about his relationship with Sabres enforcer Rob Ray.

Like, why did two close friends want to hit each other so often?

The two had traded punches on golf courses, in watering holes, in locker rooms and at practices.

All in good fun, of course.

Their most publicized clash occurred in the living room of the apartment they shared in Buffalo.

They were watching TV one evening when Ray flicked on the Discovery Channel. Barnaby grabbed the remote control and switched to MTV.

"He ended up going through the Venetian blinds and the screen in the window," Ray said. "It got pretty rough."

A few of Barnaby's teeth found a new address, too.

Not that it soured the friendship.

"What would happen was, we would beat on each other for a while, then we'd go and buy each other beers," Barnaby said. "It was that kind of relationship, one of those brotherly types of things. We'd try to kill each other, but we still liked each other."

UNLUCKY MAN

If he'd walked under a ladder or gotten some bad news from a palm reader, Martin Straka might have understood.

As it was, he couldn't fathom why such an incredible string of bad luck befell him beginning in November of 2001.

First, Straka sustained a broken right leg in a game against the Florida Panthers. Four months later, he returned to the lineup against the Los Angeles Kings, and on his second shift sustained a broken orbital/sinus bone when goalie Johan Hedberg inadvertently struck him with his goal stick.

"He's not the luckiest guy on our team," Hedberg allowed.

Straka could have called it quits for the season, but like some character out of a Monty Python movie, he returned a few weeks later against the Carolina Hurricanes.

On his sixth shift, he whiffed on a pass and caught his skate in a rut, re-opening the crack in his leg.

It would get worse.

Straka was at home training in the Czech Republic that summer, two days away from skating again, when he was attacked by a 300-pound barbell.

A weight machine shifted, causing Straka to lose his grip on the barbell. He fell and was pinned under the barbell. Teammate Milan Kraft pulled him from the wreckage.

Straka sustained a chipped vertebra and ligament damage in his back. He feared season-ending surgery but escaped that fate and resumed his career early that season.

Not before one more scare, though.

He was skating laps during a morning workout when—incredibly—he ran into Hedberg's stick again.

The twist was that Hedberg was neither holding the stick nor anywhere near it. It was sitting atop the net. Straka left the ice bleeding.

That night, Straka, sporting a band-aid on his forehead, saw a reporter approaching him.

"Stay away from me," he joked. "Something bad might happen."

JESSE JAMES

Philadelphia Flyers defenseman Luke Richardson outraged Penguins fans in Game 5 of a 2000 playoff series, when he blasted a puck from relatively short range at Penguins defenseman Bob Boughner, striking him in the chest.

Boughner, who was wrestling Flyers forward Keith Jones, went down like he'd been shot.

Penguins coach Herb Brooks verbally tore into Richardson the next day.

"I'd go back in his family tree," Brooks said. "Maybe he's a direct descendant of the guy that shot Jesse James in the back. You know, the coward that shot Jesse James in the back. It must be in his family tree. There's a code for tough guys in the league. This was way past the code."

WHO'S THE WHITE-HAIRED GUY?

Former Penguins coach Ivan Hlinka, a native of Czechoslovakia, had so much trouble communicating with his players that he let assistant coach Rick Kehoe do most of the talking.

One night in Minnesota, defenseman Marc Bergevin decided to play a joke on Hlinka, who could often be found smoking a cigarette near the Zamboni machine between periods and after games.

Bergevin went up to a security guard and said, "The white-haired guy who is outside smoking, he's not with us."

The security guard approached Hlinka and said, "Excuse me, sir, you have to leave."

Replied Hlinka: "Why?"

Security guard: "You can't be here. You gotta go."

Hlinka: "I'm the coach."

Security guard: "No, no, you have to go."

The guard finally gave in, only because players began laughing uncontrollably.

MOOSE ON THE LOOSE

The 27-year-old goalie with the blue mask was thought to be a throw in when the Penguins made an apparently minor trade with the San Jose Sharks on March 12, 2001.

Within weeks, Johan "Moose" Hedberg was a folk hero.

In his debut, he stopped Florida Panthers star Pavel Bure on two of three breakaways—and it was all uphill from there.

Hedberg's mask featured a big blue moose head. His previous team was the minor-league Manitoba Moose.

Incredibly, Hedberg took the Penguins all the way to the Eastern Conference final against the New Jersey Devils, outdueling Olaf Kolzig and Dominik Hasek along the way.

An old Penguin named Olie Sundstrom had helped Hedberg to develop his puck-handling skills back in Sweden (the two used to

Martin Straka's unfathomable run of bad luck began with a broken leg on October 28, 2001. *(Photo by James M. Kubus/Pittsburgh Tribune-Review)*

watch video of Philadelphia's Ron Hextall), and former Penguins defenseman Randy Carlyle coached him in the minor leagues.

Penguins fans wore foam antlers to playoff games that season.

UNLIKELY HERO

The Penguins' second-round playoff series against the Buffalo Sabres in 2001 went to overtime in Game 7.

If somebody had gone into the Penguins dressing room at the point and picked the most unlikely player to score, defenseman Darius Kasparaitis would have been near the top of the list.

Kasparaitis had one goal in 56 playoff games.

But, sure enough, a little more than halfway through the period, he took a pass from Robert Lang at the edge of the left circle and ripped a wrist shot toward legendary goaltender Dominik Hasek.

It went in.

"I can't believe I did that," Kasparaitis said later.

The moment the puck hit twine, Kasparaitis sprinted to center ice and did a belly flop, kicking his legs in the air like an Olympic swimmer.

"I usually kick my feet when I get hurt," he said. "The last time I did it was when I got hit with the puck in the face."

Players were in shock in a delirious Penguins dressing room.

"I haven't seen him score a goal in practice since I've been here," said veteran winger Kevin Stevens, who had rejoined the team three months earlier in a trade. "He's got the worst wrist shot in hockey."

QUOTABLE

Like his Finnish forebearer Ville Siren, Ville Nieminen was a deliciously quotable Penguin. As teammate Randy Robitaille put it, "He always had something to say."

Often, it was something worth pondering, if only for a few seconds.

A sampling of Nieminen-isms:

- On a stretch of good play: "Let's not go building any kind of cloud homes or skyscrapers or something like that. It's just two games."
- On chatting up opponents: "I don't know how they could understand my language. It's Finglish."

- On his stretch of minus games: "Playing like that—having a green jacket at minus-11—is unacceptable."
- On Alexei Kovalev's pinpoint shot that beat Buffalo one night: "You don't even want to celebrate on a goal like that. That was from somewhere else. That guy comes out of some other league, some better league."
- On losing Kovalev in a trade: "There's a hole in the highway. Every player has to chip in a little bit of sand from his own pocket, so we can fill it and keep going."

BROKEN GLASS

Left winger Ville Nieminen arrived at training camp in 2002 in excellent shape.

Well, except for those nasty scars on his arms and legs.

Ivan Hlinka was the first Czech-born, NHL coach. *(Photo by James M. Kubus/Pittsburgh Tribune-Review)*

Nieminen nearly saw a summer's worth of training go down the drain—literally—when he fell through a sauna door at his home in Finland.

A loose stair caused Nieminen to slip. He crashed legs-first through the sauna's glass door.

"The big door was in 50,000 little pieces," he said. "It looked like somebody got killed in the sauna. There was so much blood that I passed out and hit my face in the glass."

Just before he passed out, Nieminen yelled to his girlfriend to call for help. Luckily, they lived next door to a firehouse.

Help arrived in less than a minute.

"It's a good place to live," Nieminen said.

Doctors needed 62 stitches to close wounds on Nieminen's legs, quadriceps, elbows and forehead.

He escaped debilitating injury and was ready for training camp.

HOCKEY REVOLUTION

Mario Lemieux's impact on Pittsburgh's hockey culture is perhaps best measured by the proliferation of indoor rinks.

When he arrived as a rookie in 1984, the area held just eight rinks, two of which were used year-round. A little more than a decade later, the number approached 30, virtually all of them year-round facilities.

HOMETOWN HERO

One of Greg Malone's truly memorable games as a Penguins centerman occurred on December 1, 1979, the day his first son, Ryan, was born.

Greg brought his wife, Diana, to the hospital on a Friday night. Their baby wasn't delivered until 4 p.m. Saturday.

With a game scheduled that night, Greg went straight from the delivery room to the arena.

"Our coach, Johnny Wilson, said, 'You want to play?'" Malone recalled. "I said, 'Sure.' During introductions, they said, 'We'd like to welcome the newest Penguin, Ryan Gregory Malone.'"

Approximately 23 years later, PA announcer John Barbero would call Ryan Gregory Malone's name again—every time he scored a goal as a Penguins rookie.

Fans went wild over Johan "Moose" Hedberg's playoff heroics in 2001.
(Photo by James M. Kubus/Pittsburgh Tribune-Review)

His dad, who had long since become the Penguins' head scout, heard a few of those calls from the press box.

In the 2003-04 season, Ryan Malone became the first Pittsburgh-born and trained player to reach the NHL. And he did it for his hometown team. He wore his dad's old No. 12 and became the first Penguins rookie to score 20 goals since Shawn McEachern in 1992-93.

"These games are like a dream come true for me," he said.

Ryan finished the year with 22 goals and 43 points, Impressive stuff, but he had a way to go to catch up to his old man on the team's all-time scoring list.

Greg Malone was 11th at the time, with 364 points (143 goals, 221 assists). He also shared the team record for assists in a game (six) with Mario Lemieux and Ron Stackhouse.

• • •

Ryan Malone's game is not very similar to his father's. The two don't share the same view on tattoos, either.

Ryan has the family crest tattooed on his back and a hornet (for his midget team) on his right arm. On his left arm is a dream catcher

A child shall lead them: Penguins center Greg Malone and wife, Diana, hold future rookie sensation, Ryan Malone, at a team Christmas party in 1981. *(Photo courtesy of the Pittsburgh Penguins)*

with Chinese words saying "Follow your dreams," and a Celtic cross with a green dragon, for good luck.

"He knows I don't like 'em, but it's a fad nowadays," Greg Malone said. "Basically, all young people have them. I'm still allowed to make my stand, though."

MY LEFT FOOT

Twice in their history, the Penguins drafted first overall. The first time, in 1984, they took a special, French-Canadian athlete named Mario Lemieux.

The second time, in 2003, they snagged French-Canadian goaltender Marc-Andre Fleury, who proved his incredible athleticism shortly after the draft, during a pool party at general manager Craig Patrick's house.

Fleury was reclining on a raft in the pool when somebody tossed him a miniature plastic ball.

He caught it with his left foot.

DEATH OF A LEGEND

The hockey world mourned on August 11, 2003, when Herb Brooks died in a one-car accident in his home state of Minnesota. He was 66.

"Herb Brooks is synonymous with American hockey, and those of us lucky enough to be around him learned something from him every day," said Penguins general manager Craig Patrick. "I knew him for more than 30 years. We played together, we coached together, and we worked together. Herbie loved the game, he lived the game, and his contributions to the Penguins over the past eight years have been immeasurable. He will be sorely missed."

Throughout his career, Brooks was intensely interested in spreading his hockey knowledge. Penguins coach Eddie Olczyk, a Chicago native who played on the 1984 US Olympic team, will never forget his last encounter with Brooks.

It occurred in Pittsburgh a month before Brooks's death, during the Penguins' rookie orientation camp.

Olczyk had just been named Penguins coach.

"One of the last things Herbie said to me was, 'Always remember that you're American-born—you can do it and do it your way,'" Olczyk said. "That's one thing I'll take with me."

Goalie Marc-Andre Fleury, drafted first overall in 2003, flanked by European scout Mark Kelley. *(Photo by James M. Kubus/Pittsburgh Tribune-Review)*

6

THE NEXT ONE

Sidney Crosby's Amazing Rookie Year

WINNING TICKET

On the morning of July 22, 2005, Pittsburgh Penguins general manager Craig Patrick made sure to stop by the majestic St. Patrick's Cathedral on Madison Avenue in Manhattan. Couldn't hurt, you know?

Patrick's team had only a 6.25-percent chance of winning the NHL's Draft Lottery later that day. Only three other teams—the Columbus Blue Jackets, the New York Rangers, and the Buffalo Sabres—had as good a chance, but 6.25 percent isn't good under any circumstance. The winning ticket would give a team the right to draft 17-year-old center Sidney Crosby, the NHL's most-celebrated prospect since Mario Lemieux 21 years earlier. By this time, Lemieux was the Penguins' owner.

Back at the Penguins' media room in Mellon Arena, reporters and team employees gathered to watch the lottery on closed-circuit television. In New York, NHL Commissioner Gary Bettman would open 29 envelopes, each with a team emblem inside. The 29th held the logo of the winner.

The scene intensified as Bettman opened the envelope. Only the Penguins and the Mighty Ducks of Anaheim were left. The next envelope held the emblem of the winner. Patrick clutched a tiny four-leaf clover—anything to please the Hockey Gods—as Bettman opened the envelope.

It was a Penguin.

The roar from Mellon Arena could be heard all the way to Cole Harbour, Nova Scotia, home of Crosby, the kid who'd racked up

120 goals and 183 assists in 121 games of junior hockey. He would make his NHL debut on October 5, which happened to be Lemieux's 40th birthday.

LIKE HOTCAKES

Crosby's impact was felt within minutes of the team winning the lottery. Mellon Arena phone lines lit up like Times Square, and ticket-office operators were asked to stay until midnight. A few days later, somebody from Australia called to order seats. By mid-August, the team had sold more tickets than in the entire previous season. This before they even launched their season-ticket marketing campaign. When single-game tickets went on sale, more than 10,000 were sold in four hours, tripling the normal first-day total.

CRYSTAL BALL

Shortly after NHL commissioner Gary Bettman opened the winning envelope on lottery day, Penguins announcer Mike Lange, who was at home, calmly prepared to check the Internet to see who'd won. Just then, a friend called and told Lange the great news: Sid "The Kid" was coming to Pittsburgh.

Lange claimed he wasn't surprised, despite the Penguins having had only a 6.25-percent chance.

"I knew it was going happen," Lange said. "I really did. It isn't something I haven't been saying for the past four or five months. I think it was destiny."

NO SLEEPOVERS

Lots of people expected Crosby to be Mario Lemieux's linemate. Very few expected him to be Lemieux's housemate. Much to the Lemieux's surprise, Crosby moved into the second floor of their suburban mansion and stayed for his entire rookie season. He and Lemieuxs' oldest son, nine-year-old Austin, hit it off, playing hockey in the driveway.

As for house rules, Lemieux said it was perfectly fine for Crosby to have girls over—with one stipulation:

"No sleepovers," Lemieux said.

Crosby's reaction?

"No comment," he said, laughing.

Sidney Crosby makes a happy arrival in Pittsburgh, with new teammate and future landlord Mario Lemieux standing behind him. *(Photo by James M. Kubus/ Pittsburgh Tribune-Review)*

And would Crosby, in fact, be required to babysit Mario and Nathalie Lemieux's four young children?

"It's not in his contract," Lemieux said. "But you never know."

FIRST IMPRESSION

A small sampling of hockey fans and Penguins employees got their first live glimpse of the 5-foot-11, 193-pound Crosby in action during an intrasquad scrimmage at training camp. He didn't disappoint.

One look at the faces of men who'd been playing and watching hockey all their lives told the story. Kevin Stevens, a Penguins star turned scout, laughed and shook his head when appraising Crosby's talent.

"Two steps and he's gone," Stevens said. "He's like a Russian-style skater."

Michel Therrien, who was coaching the Penguins' farm team at the time but soon would replace Eddie Olczyk behind the Penguins bench, said, "I sit here in my seat like a fan when that kid's on the ice."

Bob Errey, the Penguins' television analyst, said simply, "He's one of the best passers I've ever seen." That was obvious when Crosby took a feed from John LeClair in the slot and feigned to shoot. Most players would have, but Crosby slid a sweet pass to Mark Recchi for a tap-in.

Recchi was one of the many former Penguins Stanley Cup winners at Mellon Arena that day. Others included, in various on- and off-ice capacities, Mario Lemieux, Stevens, Troy Loney, Phil Bourque, Errey, and assistant coaches Randy Hillier and Joe Mullen.

They all liked what they saw.

MR. POPULAR

Crosby arrived in the NHL with more endorsement opportunities than most players amass in a career, easily surpassing his $850,000 base salary with money made off the ice.

"He's like God north of the border," said Len Rhodes, the Montreal-based vice president of Global Marketing for Reebok Hockey, which signed Crosby to a multiyear deal. "And I know he'll be big south of the border."

Before Crosby set foot in training camp, Reebok had sold more than 16,000 of his No. 87 jerseys. (Crosby wears that number because his birth date is 8/7/87.) What's more, Crosby's Web site, www.crosby87.com was absorbing more than 100,000 hits per day, and he was pitching Gatorade, Reebok, Telus—one of Canada's leading telecommunications companies—and Sherwood. He'd already guest-starred on *The Tonight Show with Jay Leno*. He had appeared shirtless in *Vanity Fair* and fully clothed in *GQ* too.

Another measurement of Crosby's crazy popularity: a Team Canada jersey he'd worn in the gold medal game at the World Junior Championships was stolen, then recovered and auctioned off for $22,100. Proceeds went to youth hockey charities and south Asian tsunami relief.

Reebok knew it was taking a chance on signing an unproven player.

"It's rare for us," Rhodes told the *Pittsburgh Tribune-Review*. "We'd only do it with someone of his caliber."

Crosby's agent, Pat Brisson, said his client took an ardent interest in the marketing realm, right down to the color of the items in Crosby's Reebok clothing line. All items are emblazoned with a SC87 icon, reflecting Crosby's initials and jersey number.

BIG SHOTS

Crosby's rookie deal with Reebok was worth a reported $2.5 million. Some predicted he'd be as big in Pittsburgh as Steelers quarterback Ben Roethlisberger, who made about $4 million off the field in his rookie season.

Getting mentioned in select company was nothing new to Crosby. Soon he would begin shooting ads for Reebok's "I Am What I Am" campaign, which included tennis star Andy Roddick, basketball star Allen Iverson, rapper 50 Cent, actress Christina Ricci, and baseball star Curt Schilling.

Not that Crosby was obsessed with marketing himself. Far from it.

"It'd be nice if the Roethlisberger thing happened to me, but I'm not worried about it," he said. "I can't get caught up worrying about other things besides hockey. I guess in a way, [marketing] is part of it. But I'm here to play hockey."

NO CREDIT

It is easy to forget that Crosby was only 17 when the Penguins drafted him. He didn't turn 18 until a month before training camp. In light of that, it makes a little more sense that he didn't know what to do with his first professional paycheck.

"I haven't seen it yet," Crosby said a few days after it was issued. "I haven't got a bank account, so I'm working on it."

Actually, he had an account back home in Cole Harbour, Nova Scotia, but hadn't yet transferred it. He didn't yet have a credit card yet, either, but soon would have all that and more, including his first vehicle—a leased Range Rover.

LIGHTS, CAMERA, ACTION

Normally, there isn't a news conference at the visiting team's hotel the day before a regular-season opener. But sure enough, the NHL arranged for Crosby and Mario Lemieux to meet the press a day before the Penguins played in New Jersey to kick off the 2005-06 season.

The Kid's debut was that big.

There aren't usually 175 media credentials issued for a regular-season game, either. That's the going number for a conference final, but there were approximately that many issued for this one.

Among the outlets covering Crosby's debut were *Newsweek*, *ET Canada*, and Global TV—a Halifax-based company that rarely covers sports but was on hand to follow native son Crosby.

"We've been covering him since he was 12," said Gray Butler, a cameraman for Global TV. "We're covering this as a news event, not a sporting event. It's about the rebirth of the NHL and about Sidney with the world on his shoulders."

Crosby recorded his first NHL point midway through the third period on a perfect pass across the goalmouth to Mark Recchi. In the opening minutes of the game, Devils goalie Martin Brodeur thwarted Crosby's first NHL shot, a point-blank backhander.

"As much as you'd like to score, you look who's in net, and it's Brodeur who just stopped you," Crosby said after a 5–1 loss. "So you just shake your head a little bit."

PARENT TRAP

About seven hours before his NHL debut, Crosby encountered a most unusual sight as he made his way from the dressing room to the team bus after the morning skate at Continental Airlines Arena.

"There's my parents," he said to a teammate, "in that scrum over there."

Indeed, Troy and Trina Crosby had been engulfed by separate packs of reporters. Somebody asked Troy about his son's recent appearance in *Vanity Fair* magazine.

"Pretty neat," he said. "People said he looked like me a little bit, so it's good."

HOME COOKIN'

Pop diva and Pittsburgh native Christina Aguilera was the surprise anthem singer at Crosby's first home game, thrilling the sellout crowd of 17,132 at Mellon Arena. Crosby made sure the thrills kept coming. At 18:32 of the second period, he scored his first NHL goal, whacking a Mark Recchi pass behind Boston Bruins goaltender Hannu Toivonen.

Fans broke into chant of "Croz-bee! Croz-bee!" after public address announcer John Barbero said, "The Pittsburgh goal . . . scored by No. 87, Sidney Crozbeeee!"

"I was happy," Crosby said. "It's something you dream about, scoring your first NHL goal. You only do it once." He finished with three points in a 7–6 overtime loss.

CANADIAN SHOOTOUT

The first shootout in Montreal Canadiens history doubled as Crosby's official "Here-I-am" moment in Pittsburgh. Every person, it seemed, among the crowd of 16,254 at Mellon Arena on November 10, 2005, stood and cheered after neither team scored in the five-minute overtime. That meant it was time for a shootout. The score was 2–2. Shootouts were new to the NHL in 2005-06, and not surprisingly, proved to be wildly popular. It's hard to dislike a breakaway contest.

Canadiens goaltender Jose Theodore stopped Mark Recchi and Mario Lemieux on the Penguins' first two attempts. Penguins goalie Jocelyn Thibault turned away Michael Ryder, Alex Kovalev, and finally, Alexander Perezhogin to set the stage for Crosby, who took off toward Theodore with a chance to win the game.

The scene was scripted perfectly. Crosby faked a forehand, then planted a missile-like backhander under the crossbar. The water bottle that had been propped atop the net flew high into the air and

Sidney Crosby shows off the puck from his first NHL goal. *(Photo by James M. Kubus/Pittsburgh Tribune-Review)*

settled to the ice like ticker tape. The arena shook like it hadn't since the 2001 playoffs.

Pittsburgh, meet your next superstar. Montreal, eat your heart out.

"Montreal was my favorite team growing up," Crosby said afterward. "I feel pretty lucky."

RAGE AND FURY

If there were any doubts about Crosby's competitive fire, they were put to rest November 16, 2005, in Philadelphia—a city where the Penguins had been intimidated many times, where they'd once gone 14 years without a victory, and where their all-time record was 17-81-8.

On this night, the Flyers' 6-foot-5, 225-pound monster defenseman, Derian Hatcher, targeted the Penguins' 18-year-old star. At 14:01 of the second period, Hatcher hammered Crosby with a high stick and forearm that broke three of Crosby's teeth. Crosby briefly left the game only to be cracked with another Hatcher high stick—this one across the neck—upon his return.

Hatcher wasn't penalized on either play. Crosby, however, was assessed an unsportsmanlike conduct for complaining. The combination of that call and Hatcher's hits lit a fuse. When Crosby came out for the third period, he skated as if a rocket pack were attached to his back. The Kid assisted on a goal and scored another to stake the Penguins to a 2–0 lead. The Flyers tied it with two late power-play goals, but Crosby won it on a breakaway with 46.7 seconds left in overtime.

When puck hit twine, Crosby, still at full speed, circled back toward his bench pumping his arms in celebration. His jersey was stained with blood.

"When stuff like that happens, you maybe try to push a little harder than normal," Crosby said, typically understating the situation. "I just wanted to make sure we got the win. I thought we deserved it."

Crosby's teammates couldn't help but be impressed.

"You see a lot of guys, they'll take one hit, one stick, and they shut it down for the rest of the game," said defenseman Brooks Orpik. "He responded great."

LOOK MA, BROKEN TEETH

It's never wise for a hockey player to get too attached to his teeth. Crosby wasn't. He just didn't expect three of them to be halved in the 21st game of his rookie season, courtesy of a high stick and forearm from Philadelphia Flyers defenseman Derian Hatcher.

Crosby's mother, Trina, was more upset than Crosby.

"She asked, 'Where's your mouthguard?'" Crosby said the next day.

As usual, Crosby had left his mouthguard in his gear bag for that particular game. He didn't plan to start wearing one because of the incident, either. Not all players are as lucky as Penguins television analyst and long-time NHL player Bob Errey, whose original teeth are intact.

"I'm not too worried about it," said Crosby, who also sustained a cut on his upper lip that required four stitches. "I pretty much realized it was eventually gonna happen. Not 20 games in, but it's happened already, so it's out of the way, and I don't have to worry about it anymore, I guess."

Crosby figured his mom would get over it. Hey, a kid loses all his first teeth. What's the big deal about losing some of the replacements?

"She knows it's part of hockey," Crosby said through a reconfigured smile.

Sidney Crosby may have lost some teeth, but the Penguins defeated the Flyers in overtime, 3-2. *(Photo by Jim McIsaac/Getty Images)*

INCREDIBLE FEAT

Crosby was the youngest player in the NHL's 89-year history to reach 100 points, the seventh rookie to hit that mark, and the only rookie to record 100 points and 100 penalty minutes. He finished with 102 points (39 goals, 63 assists) and 110 penalty minutes. He joined Hall of Fame forward Dale Hawerchuk of the Edmonton Oilers (103 points, 1981-82) as the only other 18-year-old to reach 100 points.

Crosby's tender age is what set his rookie year apart from so many others is sports history. Joe Thornton, the 2005-06 NHL scoring champion, had seven points in 55 games as an 18-year-old. Tampa Bay's Vincent Lecavalier had 28 points in 82 games.

NBA star Kobe Bryant averaged 7.6 points when he was 18. Baseball Hall of Famer Robin Yount batted .250. Cleveland Cavaliers star LeBron James put up 20.9 points per game his rookie season, but he turned 19 two months into it.

No one, least of all Crosby, expected a 100-point season. Did he meet his own expectations?

"In a way, to a certain point," he said. "I wanted to come in here and get comfortable right away and adjust as well as I could. I think I did that. But as far as the winning side of it, I don't think I could accept not winning. It's not something I want to get used to. Individually, I was pretty happy with the way things went. But on the other side of it, I want to win.

"I'd probably trade a few of those [points] for some wins and a playoff spot."

THE NEXT ONE

When Crosby was 15, a reporter from the *Arizona Republic* asked Wayne Gretzky if there was any young player out there who could break his records. "Yes, Sidney Crosby," The Great One replied. "He's the best player I've seen since Mario Lemieux." That statement added some serious fuel to the Crosby legend and led to some labeling him The Next One.

Ironic, then, that Gretzky snubbed Crosby when it came time to choose the 2006 Canadian Olympic team. Crosby didn't complain, but Gretzky, who ran Team Canada, no doubt regretted the move. The veteran-laden Canadian team did not medal in Torino, Italy, and Crosby finished his rookie season third among Canadian-born scorers with 102 points.

Another young player left off the Olympic team, Carolina's Eric Staal, finished the season with 100 points.

WASN'T MEANT TO BE

The Old Man and the Kid. Mario Lemieux and Sidney Crosby. They were supposed to make sweet music together for at least a year, skating on the same power play and perhaps even the same line. When the Penguins won the draft lottery, that was a major part of the story, but it didn't have a happy ending.

The two combined directly on only one goal—albeit a beauty—on November 3 at Nassau Coliseum in Long Island. Lemieux threaded a pass from just inside the blue line that Crosby deflected high into the net for a power-play goal at 4:01 of the third period of a 5–1 victory. It marked the first two-goal game of Crosby's career.

Crosby and Lemieux played in just 26 games together, only a handful of those on the same line. They had points on the same goal only eight times before Lemieux retired in January because of an irregular heartbeat.

At one point during his retirement news conference, Lemieux's eyes welled as he turned to his teammates, 10 of whom were rookies, and said, "All I can say to the young players is, 'Enjoy every moment of it. Your career goes by very quickly.'"

Despite his tender age, Crosby seemed to have an appreciation for Lemieux's words. He lamented the fact that the two shared so little ice together, but added, "It makes us all realize how fortunate we are to be playing."

SLEEP TALKER

Crosby received a New Year's gift when gregarious winger Colby Armstrong was recalled from the minors. The two became fast friends; road roommates; and, eventually, linemates.

Armstrong's sense of humor helped lighten the load on Crosby. Sometimes, that could even mean Armstrong taking a good-natured shot at Crosby's thick lips.

"He has a good sense of humor," Armstrong said. "You can rip on him a little bit, and he takes it really well. He doesn't get too wrapped up in a lot of stuff."

As for Crosby's habits on the road, Armstrong said his roomie likes to stretch a lot, usually goes to bed early—and talks in his sleep.

"He does that quite a bit, talks about hockey," Armstrong said. "The odd time he'll spit something out, and I don't even know what the heck it means. I try to keep it going, talking to him, but he doesn't wake up."

CONSTANT ADVERSITY

Throughout his rookie season, Crosby insisted he had arrived in Pittsburgh without any expectations. Good thing, because they would have been shattered fairly quickly.

Among the unexpected events:

- The abrupt retirements of two linemates (Ziggy Palffy and Mario Lemieux)
- A coaching change (Michel Therrien replaced Eddie Olczyk after the team's 8-17-6 start.)
- A system change
- A position change (Olczyk had Crosby playing left wing.)
- Lemieux stepping down as team CEO and putting the franchise up for sale
- A terrible team (The Penguins finished with the second-worst record in the NHL.)
- The firing of Hall of Fame general manager Craig Patrick two days after the season finale in Toronto.

Through it all, Crosby never showed signs of breaking under the pressure. The season ended the way it began—with a media horde surrounding a composed and smiling Crosby.

"I came in pretty open-minded and just tried to go with the flow and enjoy it," he said. "I think sometimes when you expect things you're caught off-guard. A lot of things happened, good and bad. Every season's like that."

But none were quite like this.

CHERRY PICKER

Controversial and immensely popular Canadian hockey analyst Don Cherry has been picking on Crosby for years.

When Crosby scored an incredible goal in the Quebec Major Junior Hockey League—he scooped the puck lacrosse style, rested it on the blade of his stick, and stuffed it into the net—Cherry ripped him on *Hockey Night in Canada.*

"I like the kid," Cherry said. "But this is a hot-dog move."

A year later, Cherry criticized Crosby for skipping a prospects All-Star game, and early in Crosby's rookie year, Cherry accused him of diving. Not long after that, Cherry was at it again, saying it was "ridiculous" that new coach Michel Therrien made Crosby an alternate captain. Cherry also implied that Crosby backed the firing of coach Eddie Olczyk.

"No kid should have as much to say as he's got to say," said Cherry, as reported by the Canadian Press. "Yapping at the referees, doing the whole thing. Golden boy."

Crosby, like millions of Canadians, had spent many a Saturday night watching Cherry during the Coach's Corner segment on *Hockey Night in Canada.* If he was bothered by Cherry's jabs, he didn't let on.

"He's always been opinionated, and I always watch Saturday night to see what he's going to say," Crosby told the *Pittsburgh Tribune-Review.* "In my case, he's mentioned my name probably not in the best of ways, but it is what it is. Everyone's entitled to their opinion. I think everyone can [read the comments] and make their own opinions. That's fine with me."

GRAND FINALE

No one who was at Mellon Arena on April 17, 2006, will forget the scene. Fans began to line up three hours before the Penguins' final home game of the season, eager for one last look at Crosby, who was three points shy of becoming the youngest player in NHL history to reach 100.

Before the game, the normally cool Crosby turned to teammate Ryan Malone and said, "I haven't been this nervous in a long time."

A standing-room-only crowd of 17,048 roared as if it were Game 7 of the Stanley Cup final, not the last home game for a miserable team that would finish with the second-worst record in the league.

Fans nearly blew the roof off the place 1:56 into the game, when Crosby assisted on an Andy Hilbert goal for his 98th point. No. 99 came at 15:19 of the second period. Twenty-five seconds after that, Crosby slipped a pass to Malone for a power-play goal and point No. 100. He was the seventh rookie in league history to reach the milestone.

Bedlam ensued.

Fans waved white T-shirts that read "Pittsburgh First," a reference to the group that was fighting to keep the Penguins in Pittsburgh. Some threw their shirts onto the ice. Penguins general manager Craig Patrick, witnessing his final game from the Mellon Arena press box, openly wept. He would be fired less than a week later.

The scoreboard flashed "Sidsational" then this: "Youngest Player in NHL History to Score 100 Points."

"It was amazing," Crosby said of the fan support. "Once I got those first two, I was just feeding off of them. I knew I couldn't leave here tonight without getting the other one. They were awesome. I'm really happy I was able to do it here."

The feeling was mutual—and the fans couldn't wait for the next chapter of Sidney Crosby's career, for with it would come the next Sidsational moment.

7
THE RISING
(2006–08)

HALF THE TEAM DOESN'T CARE

Spontaneous combustion? Hardly. The rant was later revealed to be premeditated.

But it was legendary, nonetheless.

"There are things in hockey you don't forget," said winger Colby Armstrong, years after the fact. "That was one of them."

"That" was new Penguins coach Michel Therrien eviscerating his team after a 3-1 loss to the Edmonton Oilers on Jan. 10, 2006.

"It's a pathetic performance," Therrien told reporters through a thick French-Canadian accent. "Half the team doesn't care. … They pretend to care, but I know they don't care."

Therrien then dissected his defense with such venom that it became Pittsburgh's version of the Jim Mora "*Playoffs!*" rant. His words are replayed on Pittsburgh radio stations to this day:

"I'm really starting to believe their goal is to be the worst defensive squad in the league—and they're doing such a great job at being the worst. They turn the puck over. They have no vision. They're soft. I've never seen a bunch of defensemen soft like this."

The outburst didn't exactly rally the troops. The Penguins lost their next seven games and 14 of 15. Eventually, though, "Iron Mike" instilled a toughness the club had long lacked.

WHAT IS THAT BOY THINKING?

Followers of Marc-Andre Fleury remember him wearing yellow goalie pads when he broke into the NHL. That changed when he

It was never hard to tell how Michel Therrien felt when he coached the Penguins. *(Chaz Palla, Pittsburgh Tribune-Review)*

received a letter from an Ottawa optometrist (and rabid Senators fan) named Dr. Janet Leduc.

Periodically, Leduc would see Fleury on television and wonder why he was wearing yellow—the color she claimed was most sensitive to the human eye. She figured players weaving through traffic had an easy target for the net.

"Every time I saw those yellow pads, I'd say, 'What is that boy thinking?'" Dr. Leduc recalled in an interview with the *Pittsburgh Tribune-Review*. "I'd wonder, 'Why doesn't someone tell him?'"

Dr. Leduc finally sent a letter to Penguins executives suggesting Fleury switch to white. Fleury, recuperating from an ankle injury, got hold of it.

"I thought about (the suggestion)," Fleury said, "and I thought, 'Maybe it's time.'"

Upon his return, Fleury ripped off 10 wins in 12 starts in white pads. He never turned back.

Oh, and he wound up beating the Senators in the playoffs that year, much to the chagrin of one Dr. Janet Leduc.

SID'S FIRST FIGHT

No, it didn't go quite as well as Mario Lemieux's first bout—the one where he beat the living daylights out of Gary Lupul—but Sidney Crosby didn't embarrass himself, either, when he dropped the gloves with Boston Bruins' defenseman (and former Penguin) Andrew Ference.

The two squared off on Dec. 20, 2007, in Crosby's 194th NHL game, after tussling in the corner at Boston's TD Garden. Crosby landed a few punches before officials broke it up.

"It's not something I'm going to make a habit of, by any means," Crosby said afterward.

Ference said his sister, a school teacher in Alberta, was horrified by the fight, even if it lasted only a few seconds.

"My friends said they wished it was a little longer," Ference said. "They wanted more punches."

UNDER COVER

Evgeni Malkin's most daring move came two months before his NHL debut.

In early August of 2006 Malkin, then 20, abandoned his Russian team (Metallurg Magnitogorsk) Cold War-style at an airport in Finland. He felt he'd been coerced into signing a contract with the team, and he badly wanted to join the Penguins—the franchise that had drafted him.

So he fled, hiding with his agents in two Helsinki apartments until he could secure his visa. He soon arrived safely on US soil and signed a Penguins contract worth $3 million annually.

GM Ray Shero's prediction: "He's going to score a lot."

MALKIN SCORES A LOT

Malkin's much-anticipated NHL debut came Oct. 18, 2006, against the New Jersey Devils—on Sidney Crosby Bobblehead Night.

All Malkin did that night was break a pane of glass with a slap shot, drop Devils winger Cam Janssen like a horsefly, and score the Penguins' only goal, shoveling a puck past Martin Brodeur, who thought he'd covered it.

A familiar sight for Penguins fans: Evgeni Malkin celebrating a goal. *(Christopher Horner, Pittsburgh Tribune-Review)*

After a lengthy review, public address announcer John Barbero made the call, above the din of a delirious crowd: "Penguins goal, his first of the season and first in the National Hockey League, scored by No. 71, Evgeni Maaaaaalkinnnnnnn!"

CLASSIC

"Picturesque" didn't begin to describe the setting at Buffalo's Ralph Wilson Stadium on Jan. 1, 2008.

"Perfect" was more like it.

Nobody knew quite what to make of the NHL's idea to play an outdoor game at a football stadium. The Penguins weren't even sure they could sell their allotment of a few thousand tickets.

But that was before tens of thousands of Penguins and Buffalo Sabres fans packed the parking lots to create a football game-like tailgating scene.

A light snow fell like ticker tape on two teams skating in classic uniforms (the Penguins in their original sky blue). An NHL-record crowd of 71,217 stood for much of the afternoon, dancing and singing—and Sidney Crosby, of all people, ended the game on a slick shootout goal.

Did somebody at NBC script this thing?

LONELY MAN

Colby Armstrong beat Buffalo goalie Ryan Miller 21 seconds into the 2008 Outdoor Game (later to be known as "The Winter Classic"), becoming the first player to score in a professional outdoor game in the United States.

Armstrong also was the only player to make two trips to the unheated penalty box at Buffalo's frigid Ralph Wilson Stadium.

"It's a cold, lonely place over there," Armstrong said. "There's no heater in the penalty box. When you're a bad guy, they don't give you much."

Sid Globe: Sidney Crosby looks up into the snow flakes at the NHL's first "Winter Classic" in Buffalo. (*Christopher Horner, Pittsburgh Tribune-Review*)

SCARY GARY

With 12 seconds left in Game 1 of the 2008 Eastern Conference quarterfinals, and the Penguins leading, 4-0, 41-year-old Gary Roberts hit Ottawa rookie Cody Bass from behind.

The Senators erupted. Defenseman Mike Commodore pinned Roberts face-first to the glass. Bass fired punches at the back of the old man's head.

They shouldn't have done that.

Because just then, "Scary" Gary broke free.

Four Senators players surrounded Roberts, who was practically frothing at the mouth. One of them, Christoph Schubert, threatened to hurt him.

"Scary" Gary Roberts rumbles through a fallen Flyer and sends his helmet flying. *(Chaz Palla, Pittsburgh Tribune-Review)*

Roberts laughed as he recounted the incident.

"I said, 'OK, I've had enough. If you want to hurt me, take that visor off,'" Roberts said.

Nothing came of it, and Roberts walked back to the dressing room amid frenzied cheers of "GAR-EE! GAR-EE!"

Teammates were convinced that if the melee hadn't been broken up, Roberts would have fought all four Senators. They knew the look. They'd seen it before.

Said winger Tyler Kennedy: "He's a very intense man."

CARING GARY

"Badger" Bob Johnson had been gone for 15 years, but his presence loomed over the Penguins' 2008 playoff series with Ottawa.

Twenty-three years earlier, Johnson, then coach of the Calgary Flames, tore into an 18-year-old hotshot named Gary Roberts in front of the entire team. He used Roberts as an example of a "non-committed" player.

"If there was one time in my career where I wish I could have been beamed up, that was it," Roberts recalled. "But when I look back, it's probably why I am the way I am."

Sufficiently motivated to prove his coach wrong, Roberts became a workout freak. He started carrying around a chin-up bar, oblivious to curious reactions when he'd put it up in the doorway of his hotel room.

Today, Roberts runs a workout facility in Toronto called the Gary Roberts High Performance Training Center.

• • •

Roberts achieved closure with Badger Bob shortly before the latter's death from brain cancer. The Flames were in Denver to play an exhibition game in the fall of 1991. Johnson sat in a wheelchair as players greeted him one-by-one.

Roberts welled up as he recalled his final turn with Badger Bob.

"I remember him grabbing my hand and saying, 'Hey, Roberts, I knew you'd make it.' I realized, at that moment, that he really cared."

Nearly 20 years later, Roberts waived a no-trade clause to join the Penguins. When he walked into the dressing room, he saw a sign prominently displayed on the wall.

It was Badger Bob Johnson's signature line: "It's a Great Day for Hockey."

GAME FOR THE AGES

At approximately 1:15 a.m., on June 3rd, 2008, a half-hour after the fifth-longest Stanley Cup final game ever played, somebody wondered why Sidney Crosby looked as if he hadn't broken a sweat.

"It's all gone," Crosby said. "No more sweat left."

The Penguins had just beaten the Detroit Red Wings, 4-3, in triple overtime to stave off elimination. Their locker room looked like a hospital ward.

Ryan Malone had blood dripping from his nose. He'd been cracked "right in the beak" by teammate Hal Gill's second-period slap shot and was sporting his second broken nose of the series. He barely missed a shift.

"Could you even breathe?" a reporter wondered.

"Out of my mouth," Malone said. "That's good enough."

TALBOT RUINS A PARTY

The champagne was literally on ice. The Stanley Cup sat in a crate outside of the Red Wings' dressing room. All of Detroit was poised for a massive party as the clock wound under 40 seconds in Game 5 of the '08 final.

Max Talbot ruined it.

The son of a construction worker, Talbot was a working-class player. He didn't exactly have hands of stone, but he wasn't the first guy you'd think to throw over the boards in a must-score scenario, either.

As the clock wound under a minute and goalie Marc-Andre Fleury headed for the bench, coach Michel Therrien played a hunch. He tapped Talbot, who rewarded him with one of the more dramatic goals in Penguins history, stuffing a rebound past Chris Osgood with 34.3 seconds left to force overtime.

"I don't know what I was doing on the ice at the end of a game like that," Talbot said, "but I was definitely happy to be there."

The Penguins lost the series, but Talbot would return a year later and score an even bigger goal.

Two of them, actually.

Brooks Orpik lowers the boom on Detroit forward Dallas Drake. *(Christopher Horner, Pittsburgh Tribune-Review)*

SYKORA CALLS HIS SHOT

Must have been quite the scene between the second and third overtimes of Game 5 of the '08 Final. Some players were hooked to IVs to stay energized. Others ate pizza and protein bars.

Petr Sykora announced he would score the winning goal.

"We were pumping each other up, and 'Sicks' stands up and says, 'I think I got one, boys,'" winger Adam Hall recalled. "Everybody starts hootin' and hollerin'. We loved it."

Bull's eye: Petr Sykora, as promised, scores winning goal in third overtime of Game 5 of 2008 Cup Final. *(Chaz Palla, Pittsburgh Tribune-Review)*

Sykora repeated his vow to between-the-benches reporter Pierre McGuire, then delivered on it with a power-play goal at 9:57 of the third overtime.

HOSSA'S HERE

With a strong nudge from owners Ron Burkle and Mario Lemieux, GM Ray Shero went out and got the best player on the market at the 2008 trade deadline—Marian Hossa of the Atlanta Thrashers.

This was something very new for a franchise that in its very recent past couldn't afford its own star players, let alone anyone else's.

It seems silly now, but some worried that Shero had mortgaged too much of the future in giving up Colby Armstrong and Erik Christensen, a future first-round pick (Daultan Leveille), and past first-rounder Angelo Esposito.

As of the end of the 2012-2013 season, neither Leveille nor Esposito had appeared in an NHL game.

The Penguins also received a "throw-in" named Pascal Dupuis, who, ironically, would become Sidney Crosby's linemate—the exact long-term role for which Hossa had been ticketed.

HOSSA'S GONE

Fans took it personally when Marian Hossa turned down several Penguins offers and signed with (gasp!) *the Red Wings,* the team that had just vanquished their Penguins in six bitterly contested games.

Hossa wouldn't take the Penguins' cash, but he delivered a money quote on his way out of town.

"When I compared the two teams," he said, "I felt like I would have a little better of a chance to win the Cup in Detroit."

Ouch. Those words had people dreaming of a rematch in which the Penguins would gain ultimate revenge.

It seemed like a pipe dream, though. The same two teams hadn't played in back-to-back Cup finals since the Canadiens and Blackhawks in the late 1970s.

Marian Hossa's last-second shot in Game 6 of 2008 Final goes wide against his soon-to-be Detroit Red Wings teammates. *(James M. Kubus, Pittsburgh Tribune-Review)*

8

BACK AT THE SUMMIT

(2009)

MESSAGE FROM MARIO

Brooks Orpik had barely rubbed the sleep from his eyes, the morning of Game 7 of the 2009 Stanley Cup Final, when he noticed a message on his cell phone.

"I remember rolling over," Orpik recalled, "and it was a text from Mario."

That would be Mario Lemieux, of course. Team owner. Hockey legend. He'd asked coach Dan Bylsma if he could send the players a supportive message. Bylsma couldn't say yes fast enough.

The following message from Mario greeted players before they ate breakfast that day:

This is a chance of a lifetime to realize your childhood dream to win a Stanley Cup. Play without fear and you will be successful! See you at center ice.

"I don't think anyone really had to say anything the rest of the day," Orpik said.

Players got the chance to personally thank Lemieux that night. At center ice. Next to the Stanley Cup.

• • •

Orpik received some other meaningful texts that day, from ex-teammates such as Gary Roberts, Ryan Whitney, and Darryl Sydor.

The one from Roberts: *I know this is your year. Everyone is doubting you. Stay with it.*

"It says a lot about those guys," Orpik said. "They had a huge effect on the guys and how professional we are. They were genuinely, really, really pulling for us."

CHANTING IN THE DARK

In the moments before Game 6 of the '09 Final, with the lights dimmed at ancient Mellon Arena and Marc-Andre Fleury stretching in the goal crease, a few hardy fans began a chant.

It spread like a juicy rumor.

Soon, some 17,000 others had joined in, creating a crescendo that pierced the darkness.

"Flurrr-ee! Flurrr-ee! Flurrr-ee!"

Penguins fans had developed a volatile relationship with their goaltender, often blaming him for losses but also encouraging him when he needed it most. He needed it before Game 6. He'd been pulled from Game 5 after allowing five goals on 21 shots.

Fleury would permit the powerful Red Wings just two goals on 50 shots in Games 6 and 7. He posted a 1.94 goals-against average and a .932 save percentage in 16 wins that spring.

At the championship parade, general manager Ray Shero made it a point to mention the incredible atmosphere before Game 6.

"When we needed you guys the most," he said from the stage, "it was absolutely the most fantastic crowd I've ever seen."

Fleury thanked them, too.

"I know sometimes I let some soft ones in, and you guys still cheered for me," he said. "So thanks a lot!"

OMEN CORNER

Something odd and riveting happened at the Penguins' morning skate the day of Game 7 of the '09 Final.

In a 2-on-1 drill with Tyler Kennedy, Sidney Crosby beat Marc-Andre Fleury to the far high corner, and the puck stuck in the top of the net, below the crossbar, twisted in the twine.

Hockey players (and coaches) being the superstitious sort, nobody touched the puck for the duration of the workout. They just left it there.

"We were admiring it," Kennedy said.

Crosby was asked if it might be a good omen.

"I hope so," he said.

It was: Max Talbot scored the Cup winner that night, putting the puck in almost the exact same spot, in the exact same net, on a 2-on-1 with Kennedy.

FRIENDS FOREVER

They met when both were 14, at a hockey camp in Burlington, Vt., and quickly became best friends as well as a formidable pair on and off the ice.

Kris Letang and Luc Bourdon teamed on defense to help Canada win two World Junior Championships.

"We were the same," Letang recalled. "We just wanted to have fun and enjoy life."

Bourdon's life tragically ended too soon. A prized Vancouver Canucks prospect, he was killed in a motorcycle accident in 2008. He was 21.

Letang had trouble coping.

"I'm always thinking about him being with me in spirit," Letang said a year later, as the Penguins were rolling toward the Cup. "I don't know what you call it in English—prayer? —but I know Luc is always there for me."

Letang's overtime goal against Washington in Game 3 of a second-round series was as big as any goal in the playoffs that year. The instant that the puck hit twine, he thought of Bourdon.

"I knew right away he was there," Letang said.

After the game, Letang received a text from Bourdon's mother, Suzanne, and girlfriend, Charlene Ward.

What did it say?

"Just, 'Good luck, we're happy for you,'" Letang said. "And, 'Nice goal.'"

SHOWDOWN

Penguins-Capitals '09 was one of the more anticipated playoff series of the modern era, billed as a showdown between "Sid The Kid" and "Alexander The Great."

It did not disappoint.

Sidney Crosby and Alex Ovechkin—long since cast as the NHL's version of Magic Johnson and Larry Bird—combined for 27 points in a series that saw more turns than the Tour de France.

The Penguins stormed back from a two-games-to-none deficit and eventually won Game 7 at Washington, 6-2.

Crosby notched the Penguins' first and last goals of Game 7. The second was drenched in symbolism. Crosby stripped Ovechkin and scored on a breakaway, and replays from behind the goal showed Ovechkin, on his knees, fading into the background as Crosby hauled toward the Washington net.

Later, somebody asked Ovechkin what he said to Sid in the hand-shake line.

"I just wished him good luck," Ovechkin said, "and told him to win the Stanley Cup."

THE PIECE

The last player in Penguins history who'd boast about himself? Might be Rob Scuderi, a mild-mannered, stay-at-home defenseman from Long Island, NY, who worked his way through the system before becoming an integral part of the Stanley Cup team of '09.

Marc-Andre Fleury stops Alex Ovechkin on a breakaway in early moments of Pens' Game 7 win at Washington. *(Chaz Palla, Pittsburgh Tribune-Review)*

"The Piece" doing what he does best: protecting his goaltender. *(Pittsburgh Penguins)*

Imagine Scuderi's horror, then, when he said the wrong word to a reporter and made himself sound like a braggart. In a published story during the Final, Scuderi meant to say he was "a piece" to the Penguins' puzzle. But he accidentally said "the piece."

When the story appeared, Scuderi had to laugh. The piece?

"It's not Sid, it's not (Evgeni Malkin)," Scuderi joked. "Apparently it's me."

Needless to say, teammates jumped on the gaffe like a turnover in the neutral zone. By the end of practice that day, Rob Scuderi was known to one and all by a new name: "The Piece."

THE CREASE

Rob Scuderi truly was indispensible during one memorable scrum near the Penguins' net in the waning seconds of Game 6 against Detroit.

Somehow, he wound up on his knees in the goal crease. He made at least two saves, as every Detroit player on the ice crashed the net. The Penguins survived to play Game 7.

"The Piece" was careful not to take too much credit for his goaltending, lest his teammates conceive an even more diabolical nickname.

"I'm more of a stand-up goalie, not a butterfly goalie," Scuderi joked. "No, I just kind of blacked out."

NICK OF TIME

If it wasn't the most dramatic save in NHL history, it belongs on the short list—and even though things were happening fast, Marc-Andre Fleury immediately identified the shooter: Nicklas Lidstrom.

That is what the 2009 Stanley Cup Final boiled down to in the manic final seconds of Game 7—Future Hall of Famer Lidstrom from the low left circle on a rebound attempt.

"Yeah, I knew it was him," Fleury recounted later. "I was like: 'Oh (expletive).'"

Sergei Gonchar and daughter Natalie enjoy Cup-winning night in Detroit. *(Chaz Palla, Pittsburgh Tribune-Review)*

Fleury explained that he normally would have extended his right leg along the ice on a rebound that kicked out to his right. But an innate sense told him there was no time, so he lunged in the air. Lucky for him, Lidstrom's shot wasn't along the ice.

Even after making the save, Fleury braced for more.

"I was scared they'd shoot again," he said, "but then I saw Jordan Staal throwing his gloves up, and I thought, 'OK, I can do it too.'"

Penguins coach Dan Bylsma looks on as President Obama hoists the Stanley Cup at the White House ceremony in 2009. *(Justin Merriman, Pittsburgh Tribune-Review)*

DAN WHO?

Everybody had the same question when the Penguins fired Michel Therrien with 25 games left in the 2008-09 season and replaced him with Dan Bylsma, coach of their minor league team in Wilkes-Barre, Pa.

Who the heck is Dan Bylsma?

A look at Bylsma's playing career provided some clues. He made up for modest talent with fierce desire and a thinking man's approach.

Once in a minor-league game with the Long Beach Ice Dogs, Bylsma went to his knees to block a shot that crushed his orbital bone. The nerve damage was such that he never regained his original smile. His face was broken in 11 places and required 115 stitches and 13 pieces of metal to mend.

How many stitches and broken bones had he sustained in his career? Bylsma said he lost count at 550 and 26, respectively.

Pretty soon, he became associated with some other numbers: 18-3-4. That was his record to end the season, easily the best 25-game start in Penguins' history and tied for second-best in NHL history.

COACH'S CORNER

Veteran winger Matt Cooke was among the Penguins who'd played against their new coach. Cooke literally had the scars to prove it.

"That's why I still wear this brace on my right knee," Cooke said, pulling up his pant leg. "He got me."

As the story goes, Cooke went to retrieve a puck in the corner, and his defenseman failed to shield him from the raging rhino that was the 6-foot-2, 215-pound Bylsma.

"I say it was a late hit," Cooke said. "He just says, 'It *might* have been a *little* late.'"

SHUT UP, PHILLY

Eddie Olczyk couldn't believe his eyes as he looked down from the broadcast booth. Bill Guerin was equally incredulous at the Penguins' bench.

Was Daniel Carcillo really going to fight Max Talbot?

The Philadelphia Flyers had just taken a 3-0 lead in the second period of Game 6 of a memorable 2009 series. A seventh game seemed inevitable. Desperate to alter the momentum, Talbot went looking for a fight.

In former teammate Daniel Carcillo, standing next to him at the faceoff, Talbot saw a possible partner, someone just dim enough to engage. He turned to Carcillo and said, "What the hell, let's go."

Guerin heard their conversation. He told Root Sports he remembered saying to himself, "There's no way Carcillo's going to get sucked into that."

Carcillo got sucked into that.

Olczyk, calling the game for NBC, immediately recognized the mistake.

"I understand why Max Talbot is fighting here, but if you're Daniel Carcillo, there's really no reason to engage," Olczyk said on the air. "You're up 3-0. Do not give the Penguins any opportunity to build some momentum off a scrap."

The Penguins built momentum off the scrap. Carcillo won the fight, all right, and implored the already delirious fans to cheer louder. But Talbot, sporting a black eye, responded with one of the iconic gestures in Penguins history: He put an index finger to his mouth, as if to say "Shhhhh," as he skated off the ice. The Penguins scored 14 seconds later and stormed back to win.

Max Talbot just lost a fight, but he tells Flyers fans to zip it—and they soon would in Penguins' legendary Game 6 win in 2009. *(Chaz Palla, Pittsburgh Tribune-Review)*

Did losing a fight really change momentum? Every member of that team will say yes, including Talbot.

The key to it all: "I was lucky enough to have Dan Carcillo beside me."

THE GENOS

En route to winning the Conn Smythe Trophy as the most valuable player of the 2009 playoffs, Evgeni Malkin was nearly upstaged by two members of his own family: his parents.

"The Genos," as they came to be known—based on Evgeni's nickname, "Geno"—were fixtures at home games. Regular people who fit right in. Their wildly enthusiastic cheering was often shown

The Genos—Vladimir and Natalia Malkin—cheer on the Penguins in the 2009 Stanley Cup Final. (Christopher Horner, Pittsburgh Tribune-Review)

on the scoreboard. Fans would migrate to their section for photos—knowing The Genos were always happy to oblige.

Malkin's parents were Pittsburghers at heart. They hailed from the Russian town of Magnitogorsk, loosely translated as "Iron City." Vladimir had been a machine inspector at Magnitogorsk Iron and Steel Works. He also played for the city's hockey team, as would Evgeni.

Natalia laughed one day as Vladimir gave the *Pittsburgh Tribune-Review* his version of how the parents had influenced the son.

"I think Evgeni took a lot from me—the way to think on the ice, the vision, my hands," Vladimir said. "But the way he is inside—the toughness and personal character—that's from his mom. She's a tough girl."

GENOS IN "JAIL"

For a while, The Genos ran their son's offbeat restaurant/deli back in Magnitogorsk, called the VIP Zone. It was designed in the motif of a maximum-security Russian prison, complete with barred windows, aluminum forks, lamps that looked like police flashlights, waitresses in striped suits, and bills dotted with fingerprints.

Malkin told a local newspaper he wanted "a restaurant that would be something absolutely new, like nothing before it."

Safe to say, the place was unique. It also closed a few years later.

STREET HOCKEY FOR THE CUP

Sidney Crosby and his buddies back in Cole Harbour, Nova Scotia, were no different than kids all over North America when it came to street hockey: They'd often play for an imaginary Stanley Cup.

This time they were playing for the real one.

Crosby's day with the Cup was Aug. 7, 2009—his 22nd birthday—and was notable for several reasons, including a parade that attracted 75,000 people.

But the coolest part had to be the high-stakes roller hockey game: Winner gets the Cup. Sid played goal, just like old times, and to nobody's surprise his team won, 7-3.

"I grew up with these guys, and since we were five or six, we played exactly the same way we did today," Crosby told the Hall of Fame. "We probably played for the Stanley Cup 500 times, whether it was snowing, raining, or dark."

ROOTING FROM AFAR

Somehow, it didn't seem right: The first homegrown Penguin was in a bar in Faribault, Minn., attending a bachelor party when the Penguins raised the Cup in Detroit.

Bill Guerin says hello to his own personal fan club—his kids—before Game 5 of the 2009 Stanley Cup Final. (Christopher Horner, Pittsburgh Tribune-Review)

Almost exactly a year earlier, Ryan Malone had been a huge part of the team's run to the Final. His final moments in black and gold were spent slumped at his locker, barely able to move after an agonizing Game 6 loss to the Red Wings.

What was it like now, watching from afar?

"You're happy for 'em, but it was weird, because you know so many of the guys, and you were in that position the year before," Malone said. "But it was nice to see them win for the fans. They were patient, and now they have the reward."

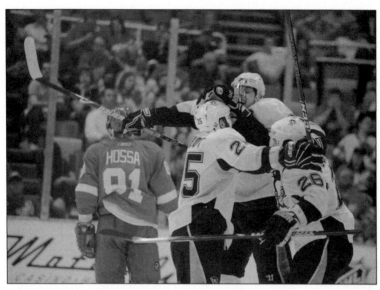

Max Talbot, Evgeni Malkin and Ruslan Fedotenko celebrate Talbot's first goal in Game 7 as a certain Red Wing skates away. *(Chaz Palla, Pittsburgh Tribune-Review)*

Marc-Andre Fleury and Sidney Crosby celebrate '09 Cup title with thousands and thousands of their closest friends. *(Pittsburgh Penguins)*

CITY OF CHAMPIONS

Barely four months after the Steelers celebrated a record sixth Super Bowl title, locals lined the streets for another parade—this time, on a gorgeous, 82-degree afternoon.

An estimated 375,000 fans converged downtown to revel in the Penguins' Game 7 win over Detroit. They lined streets 20-deep in spots, leaned out of office windows, and stood atop multi-level parking garages to catch glimpses of the players and the Cup.

Pittsburgh once again was The City of Champions.

One of the biggest roars was for winger Bill Guerin, who'd lent leadership and goal-scoring ability at the trade deadline. Guerin was about to become an unrestricted free agent. When he stepped up to the podium, fans chanted, "One more year! One more year!" He would indeed sign for one more year.

Taking it all in, one couldn't help but think of a certain Red Wings forward who'd left Pittsburgh for Detroit the previous summer.

One fan made a sign especially for him:
"HOSSA, ARE YOU WATCHING?"

Long-time PA announcer John Barbero died July 26, 2010, of a brain tumor. A familiar and friendly face at Penguins games for nearly 40 years, Barbero was 65. His last game, fittingly, was Game 6 of the 2009 Stanley Cup Final, one of the memorable home games in Penguins history. The team honored Barbero with a Stanley Cup ring shortly thereafter. *(Pittsburgh Penguins)*

9

HOCKEY HOTBED

(2010–13)

ONE-SHOT DEAL

Brent Johnson would trade a shutout for a knockout every time.

On February 2, 2011, at Consol Energy Center, fisticuffs broke out between the Penguins and Islanders with 16 seconds left in regulation and the Penguins leading 3-0. Nothing unusual about that—until Johnson removed his goalie mask, skated down the ice, and challenged Islanders goalie Rick DiPietro to a fight.

Much to his regret, DiPietro obliged.

Johnson opened (and closed) the bout with a left hook Smokin' Joe Frazier would have been proud of. DiPietro was flat on his back, stunned, when he looked up at Johnson with a question.

"He said, 'Are you a lefty?' Johnson recalled. "I said, 'No, Rick, no I'm not.'"

DiPietro wound up with a broken jaw. Johnson had a story to tell his grandchildren. So it hardly mattered that he lost credit for the shutout because he missed the final 16 seconds. It was a trade he'd make every time.

• • •

When the teams met nine days later on Long Island, Johnson and his teammates might as well have worn bull's eyes instead of numbers. The Islanders, still seething over the Penguins' joyous reaction to Johnson's knockout, ambushed them at every turn.

In a game that hearkened to the bench-clearing-brawl days of the 1970s, the teams combined for 346 penalty minutes, 20 miscon-

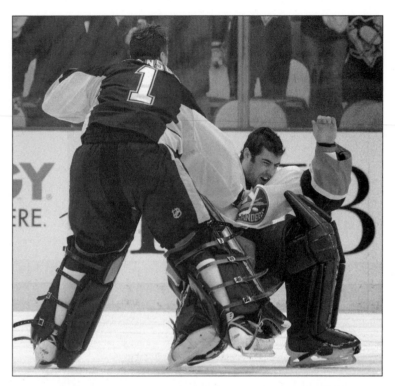

Brent Johnson (1) drops Rick DiPietro with a short left. *(Gene J. Puskar, AP Images)*

ducts, 15 fighting majors, and 10 ejections. At one point, a fence between the dressing rooms was shut during a hallway lockdown.

The NHL fined the Islanders $100,000 and suspended two of their players. That hardly appeased Penguins owner Mario Lemieux, who released a statement.

It read, in part: "Hockey is a tough, physical game, and it always should be. But what happened on Long Island wasn't hockey. It was a travesty. It was painful to watch the game I love turn into a sideshow like that."

GOODBYE IGLOO

The Montreal Canadiens had beaten the Penguins in the first game ever played at the Civic (later Mellon) Arena, so maybe it was fitting they won the last game there, too.

The Canadiens stunned the Penguins, 5-2, in Game 7 of a 2010 second-round series, shutting the doors on the 49-year-old building and ruining the Penguins' chance to win back-to-back Cups.

Game 7's at The Igloo never were kind to the Penguins. They won just two of eight.

To their credit, the Penguins did not miss the moment, despite their bitter defeat. Once the handshake line cleared, they gathered near the runway to the dressing room and raised their sticks to salute the crowd.

Sidney Crosby raised his stick highest of all, then tapped it on the ice as fans in that corner cheered the vanquished champions.

HELLO CONSOL

Only the high priest of Penguins hockey could perform this baptism.

When the lights came on for the first regular-season game at the $321 million Consol Energy Center—11 years removed from the Penguins' declaration of bankruptcy—Mario Lemieux stood at center ice looking especially regal in a dark suit and purple tie.

Can you dig it? Penguins officials, including team president David Morehouse (far left) and owner Mario Lemieux (third from left) enjoy groundbreaking ceremony for Consol Energy Center. (James M. Kubus, Pittsburgh Tribune-Review)

As the sellout crowd of 18,289 roared, Lemieux raised a small bottle toward the roof. It was filled with melted ice from old Mellon Arena. He poured its contents onto the new ice surface, honoring past and present, then dropped the ceremonial first puck with NHL Commissioner Gary Bettman, who credited Lemieux and co-owner Ron Burkle with saving the team.

"They believed in this franchise," Bettman said. "We always knew Pittsburgh was a hockey town."

Tyler Kennedy scored the first Penguins goal 44 seconds into the third period. It wasn't enough in a 3-2 loss to the Flyers, but the lasting image from that night will be of Mario and his magic potion.

FLYING MONKEYS

It looked like something out of "The Wizard of Oz."

Chris Kunitz scored a hat trick against the Islanders on March 10, 2013, at Consol Energy Center, an accomplishment normally feted with flying hats. This time, it begat flying monkeys—miniature "sock monkeys" to be precise. The items had been given away at the door.

Mario Lemieux christens the ice surface at Consol Energy Center with water saved from melted ice at Mellon Arena. (James M. Kubus, Pittsburgh Tribune-Review)

Some players, even after the game, still were perplexed. When a reporter told defenseman Mark Eaton the items he'd shoveled into a pile on the ice were "sock monkeys," he cocked his head and said, "Sock monkeys, huh? I still have no idea what they are. I thought they looked a little bit like monkeys. But I still didn't know."

Just then, Canadian teammate Matt Cooke chimed in, wondering how in the world Eaton hadn't heard of sock monkeys. Eaton laughed and said, "Are they a Canadian thing?"

A sock monkey. *(Joe Starkey)*

RAY SHERO'S BIRTH STORY

Ed Johnston, who would become the Penguins' coach much later, did some masterful match-making in 1957 with his junior team in Shawinigan Falls, Quebec—and it had nothing to do with line combinations.

Rather, Johnston, then a goaltender in the Montreal Canadiens' organization, introduced teammate/assistant coach Fred Shero to the sister of a woman he was dating.

Shero, who would become a Philadelphia Flyers coaching legend, fell in love at hello.

"Fred told me after their first date, 'I'll marry that girl,'" Johnston recalled. "And it wasn't long before he did."

Five years later, Fred and Mariette Shero had a son named Rejean, or Ray, who would one day win a Stanley Cup as Penguins general manager (with E.J. on his staff).

"If it wasn't for me, Ray wouldn't be here," Johnston recalled, laughing.

Said Shero: "He never lets me forget it."

CRANKSHAFT'S BEER TAP

Penguins fans were thrilled when GM Ray Shero acquired linebacker-like defenseman Douglas Murray at the trade deadline in 2013. Their respect for Murray only grew when they learned he'd invented a beer tap.

It's true: Murray and two college buddies back at Cornell University had devised a hands-free, three-pronged keg tap they later marketed to great success.

Murray wasn't surprised when the topic arose on his first day as a Penguin.

"That story follows me along," he said, smiling. "It was a long time ago. I guess it took a bit too long to get beer in college, so we invented a quicker way to get it."

● ● ●

The other topic that arose was Murray's nickname: Crankshaft. How did he get that?

"Never will be told," he said. "I've had so many nicknames. The one that actually stuck was Crankshaft, and it turned into 'Cranky,' which I don't like, because I'm not a cranky person."

BERRY'S REGRET

Bob Berry was among several ex-Penguins coaches who attended a golf outing before the 2009-10 season.

Known to be a bit irritable during his coaching days, Berry had long since mellowed. And he marveled at how things had changed since he coached Mario Lemieux in Lemieux's rookie season of 1984-85.

"If I'd known he was going to be the owner," Berry said, "I would have been a helluva lot nicer to him."

SID HITS HOMERS

Sure, he's always dangerous with a stick in his hands. But onlookers couldn't have been expecting much when Sidney Crosby stepped to the plate for batting practice in September of 2010, during the Penguins' field trip to PNC Park.

That was before he smashed a belt-high pitch 370 feet into the right-field bleachers.

"It was halfway up the deck above the Clemente Wall," said former Pirates first baseman Sean Casey. "Pretty impressive."

SID PLAYS GOAL

The new kid in goal looked pretty good. Stopped every shot (OK, the one shot he faced). Didn't say a word.

Imagine if the players had known it was Sidney Crosby behind the mask.

It happened in December of 2012. Crosby had time on his hands because of the NHL lockout. A friend invited him to play dek hockey at Dek Star, just north of Pittsburgh. Somehow, Crosby stayed anonymous until the final buzzer.

"The ref came in and said, 'I see they got a new goalie,'" Crosby said. "Nobody else knew. I had a blast."

SID SEES SMALL ANIMALS

Crosby's personal trainer, Andy O'Brien, marvels at the man's vision more than anything else.

"He has an incredible ability to track and see things," O'Brien told 93.7 The Fan. "A lot of times we're at his place in Halifax, at the lake, and he can see across this lake, which is basically a mile wide. He can track animals in the woods, in the bushes, and see little far-off things in the grass when we're walking by—things very few other people could see.

"I really think that lends itself to his special abilities as a hockey player."

MARIO IMMORTALIZED

Mario Lemieux turned a lot of defensemen into statues during his career. On March 7, 2012, the Penguins turned Lemieux into one, accompanied, fittingly, by two New York Islanders D-men.

"This statue," said Penguins president and CEO David Morehouse, "will be an everlasting tribute to his legacy."

Lemieux said "no" to the project five times, but fellow owner Ron Burkle insisted. The Penguins commissioned California sculptor Bruce Wolfe, who produced a 10¼-foot high, 4,700-pound bronze creation christened "Le Magnifique."

Based on a 1988 *Sports Illustrated* photo and situated adjacent to Consol Energy Center, the statue depicts Lemieux splitting defensemen Rich Pilon and Jeff Norton.

The Mario Lemieux statue depicts Lemieux splitting two Islanders defensemen. *(Gene J. Puskar, AP Images)*

Pilon, incidentally, had no issue being immortalized as a prop, even if it is his rear end that is most prominently displayed.

"To tell you the truth, it's very cool," Pilon told TSN. "If you're going to get beat on a play, and it's there for everyone to see forever, it might as well be Mario."

• • •

Mario memories were flying the day of the statue unveiling. Penguins coach Dan Bylsma had a less-than-pleasant one from his days with the L.A. Kings, when his line (including Ray Ferraro and Eddie Olczyk) was assigned to "mirror" Lemieux at the old LA Forum.

They're lucky they didn't wind up on a statue.

"I believe before 30 minutes were up, we were minus-3," Bylsma said. "That experiment didn't go so well."

WINTER CLASSIC TURNS UGLY

Nobody thought much of the hit at the time.

Maybe that was because it happened behind the play, or because Sidney Crosby returned for the third period, or because there was so much giddiness going around the night of the first outdoor hockey game played at Heinz Field, including Jordan Staal's first appearance in eight months.

But make no mistake, David Steckel's blindside head shot on Crosby late in the second period will never be forgotten. It altered Crosby's career.

"He got my head, for sure," Crosby said after the game. "Maybe it was so far behind the play the officials didn't see it."

Steckel, a Washington Capitals forward, insisted the hit was not intentional. Some in the Penguins organization thought otherwise.

In any case, Crosby suited up four days later and sustained a hit from behind against Tampa Bay, smashing his head into the glass. That sent him on a concussion-recovery odyssey that robbed him of more than a full season.

Some feared Crosby's brain had become the injury equivalent of Mario Lemieux's back: a recurring problem that would shorten his career.

Like Lemieux, however, Crosby never needed much warmup time. In his first 58 post-concussion games, he rang up 93 points.

NO HE DIDN'T

Brooks Orpik hadn't scored in any of his 77 previous playoff games, so there was little reason to believe he'd be the hero as the Penguins went to overtime in Game 6 of a 2013 first-round series against the Islanders.

Uh-oh: Sidney Crosby crumples to the ice after a hit from Washington's David Steckel during Winter Classic at Heinz Field. *(Chaz Palla, Pittsburgh Tribune-Review)*

Sure enough, though, Orpik found his inner Darius Kasparaitis. He beat Evgeni Nabokov through traffic from the left point to clinch the series. It was the Penguins' most unlikely playoff winner since Kasparaitis scored on Dominik Hasek 12 years earlier.

Tyler Kennedy nearly killed Orpik during the celebration, sacking him like a defensive end.

"I think a lot of us had a delayed reaction, couldn't really tell if it went in after it hit the post," Orpik said. "You kind of just black out for a second. I certainly do, 'cause that doesn't happen to me very often. I think (Kennedy) was jumping on me before I was completely sure it was even in."

Orpik didn't even get to keep the puck.

"I tried to," he said, "and (coach) Dan (Bylsma) took it from me."

Bylsma had good reason: He wanted the puck prominently displayed in a wall encasement inside the dressing room. There, it

Mario Lemieux and Sidney Crosby didn't get much time on the ice together, but they have provided Penguins fans with countless magical moments. *(Pittsburgh Penguins)*

would reside with distinction among other special pucks given to Penguins players.

It would be the most unlikely puck of all.

JAGR WATCH

Jaromir Jagr's heart was in Pittsburgh. The rest of him never arrived.

It appeared in the summer of 2011 that the 39-year-old Jagr—a free agent after playing in Russia—would return to Pittsburgh to put a storybook ending on his career.

Mario Lemieux wanted it to happen. Most Penguins fans wanted it to happen. And it certainly appeared as though Jagr wanted it to happen. His agent, Petr Svoboda, was quoted as saying Jagr's "heart is in Pittsburgh."

The *Pittsburgh Tribune-Review* reported that the Penguins, in anticipation of Jagr's arrival, had constructed special pages and video montages on their website.

But as free agency approached, other teams joined the mix. Rumors swirled. Jagr could not be located. Fans called radio shows claiming they'd spotted him in airports. Others said he was en route from the Czech Republic to New York, and it just so happened that such a flight had been delayed when 150 turtles crawled across the runway at Kennedy International Airport (really).

The one scenario nobody had concocted was the unthinkable one that transpired: Jaromir Jagr in a *Flyers jersey*. Just hours after free agency commenced, he signed in Philly for one year and $3.3 million. Svoboda never got back to the Penguins on their $2 million offer.

Talk-show lines lit up like pinball machines.

TRAITORS?

Stanley Cup hero Max Talbot joined the Flyers on the very same day as Jagr.

Was this really happening?

Fans immediately circled the date of the Flyers' first trip to Pittsburgh: Dec. 29. They directed most of their vitriol at Jagr that night—Talbot received an ovation and a nice video tribute—but things quieted down fast: Jagr and Talbot each scored in a 3-2 Flyers win.

Fans were ready when Jaromir Jagr returned to Pittsburgh in, of all things, a Flyers jersey. (Chaz Palla, Pittsburgh Tribune-Review)

That would be a sign of things to come: The Flyers would eliminate the Penguins in six games in the first round of the playoffs.

• • •

Jagr never regretted the move. He likely would not have found a role to suit him in Pittsburgh. The Penguins were so loaded with offensive players that Sidney Crosby wound up on the second power play in the series against Philly.

"They can't even have Sid on the power play," Jagr told the *Pittsburgh Tribune-Review*. "Where would they put me?"

Going against Jagr became a blight of spring for the Penguins. He landed in Boston the next season and made one of the biggest plays in the Bruins' sweep, hooking Evgeni Malkin in overtime to set up Boston's winning goal in Game 3.

MARCH OF THE PENGUINS

When the Chicago Blackhawks opened the lockout-shortened 2012-13 season by going a record 24 games without losing in regulation, it figured to be the streak of the year in the NHL.

Then along came the Penguins, who went all of March without losing a game of any kind.

The Penguins won all 15 games that month, becoming the first team in NHL history to post a perfect month of 10 or more games. Their streak tied them with the 1981-82 Islanders as second-longest in NHL history, two behind the 1992-93 Penguins.

What made it even more remarkable was the fact that Evgeni Malkin missed 10 games. The Penguins allowed just 26 goals in 15 games and finished with three straight shutouts. They finally lost on April 2, dropping a 4-1 decision to the Buffalo Sabres.

IGINLA!

The shocking news arrived via a simply worded tweet from the Penguins:

"BREAKING NEWS: #Pens acquired Jarome Iginla from Calgary for Ben Hanowski, Kenny Agostino and 2013 first-round pick."

Whaaaat?!?

The hockey world had gone to bed believing the Boston Bruins were about to acquire Iginla, a Calgary Flames legend and the best of the "rental players" available at the 2013 trade deadline.

Those same people woke up to a Twitter frenzy. The Penguins, as GM Ray Shero put it, were "all in," having acquired Iginla, Douglas Murray, and Brenden Morrow at the trade deadline. They were also in the midst of a 15-game winning streak.

• • •

Iginla didn't play poorly with the Penguins, but the season ended on a bitterly ironic note in Boston, of all places, where the Penguins were swept in four games.

First, the series-losing goal was a slap shot that deflected off Iginla's stick. Second, Iginla was stopped on a potential game-tying shot at the buzzer in Game 4.

Did losing to Boston compound the pain of falling short of the Cup final?

"It doesn't make it easier," he said.

WEIRD WEDDING

Jordan Staal got married and "divorced" on the same day.

Ray Shero once said he would never trade Staal. He eventually had little choice. By the summer of 2012, Staal was heading into the final year of his contract. He made it clear he wanted a larger role than that of No. 3 center.

Shero could not offer a larger role, because his first two centers—some guys named Crosby and Malkin—were pretty good. Still, the Penguins offered Staal a 10-year, $60 million deal. When he turned it down, Shero knew he must act.

On the first day of the NHL Draft—in Pittsburgh —a trade was announced: Staal to Carolina, where he would be united with brother Eric, in exchange for center Brandon Sutter, defensive prospect Brian Dumoulin, and the eighth pick (defenseman Derrick Pouliot) of the draft.

Oh, and this happened to be Jordan Staal's wedding day, an event many of his suddenly former teammates were attending.

"It was a little bit awkward," conceded Brooks Orpik.

YOU HAVE TO BE HERE TO BELIEVE IT

Nobody was calling Pittsburgh a hockey hotbed in 2004.

The year before a lockout wiped out the 2004-05 season, the Penguins finished last in the NHL in attendance, averaging a paltry 11,877 fans per game. People wondered if the franchise would relocate—and how many would care if it did?

But thanks to a new superstar (Sidney Crosby), a new arena, and a talented group of first-round picks, the Penguins took off like never before. By 2013, they had sold out six straight seasons (their streak nearing 300 games) and were posting the best local television ratings of any NHL or NBA team. Folks began to wonder if the Penguins might someday threaten the hallowed Steelers as the most popular sports act around.

Traditionally a football region, Western Pennsylvania now claims 40 skating rinks, compared to a handful when Mario Lemieux arrived 30 years earlier. More than 10,000 people are participating in amateur hockey.

As the summer of 2013 began, two Pittsburgh natives—Chicago Blackhawks winger Brandon Saad and Boston Bruins defenseman Matt Bartkowksi—were competing for the Stanley Cup.

Another Steel City native, John Gibson had just led the United States to a World Junior championship. He was one of four Pittsburgh natives on the team. Four Pittsburgh-area players were selected in the 2012 draft.

This was a train moving full speed ahead.

10

UPHEAVAL

(2014-15)

STRANGE DAY, INDEED

I t might have been the most bizarre news conference in Penguins history.

When the team invited media to the Consol Energy Center on the morning of May 16, 2014—fresh off a fifth straight playoff flameout—everyone knew what was coming: the end for GM Ray Shero and coach Dan Bylsma. Several news outlets reported as much.

So when CEO David Morehouse opened with, "We're announcing that Ray Shero has been relieved of his duties," nobody was surprised.

When minutes passed without mention of Bylsma, everybody was surprised.

Even Bylsma knew he was cooked. Where was the announcement? The ensuing Q&A was the stuff of legend.

On the second question, just as a reporter started speaking, Morehouse jumped in and said, "First of all, I read on Twitter it was your birthday, but you can't believe everything on Twitter. Is it your birthday?"

Reporter: "Appreciate it, David."

Morehouse: "OK."

Was the Twitter reference a shot at erroneous reports of Bylsma's firing? Nobody knew.

Another reporter piped up: "Just to be a hundred percent clear here, you have not fired Dan Bylsma?"

Morehouse: "That's correct, we have not fired Dan Bylsma."

Reporter: "Is there an element of weirdness to that?"

Morehouse: "I don't think there's an element of weirdness. . . . We don't need to completely clean house right away."

To this day, it's unclear why Bylsma was retained only to be canned immediately upon the hiring of GM Jim Rutherford, who never met with him.

People left the news conference shaking their heads, wondering if the Penguins knew what the heck they were doing.

Turned out they did.

JIM DANDY

David Morehouse was doing his due diligence, calling around the league about prospective GMs.

In late May of 2014, he dialed up Jim Rutherford, who'd just finished a 22-year run with the Carolina Hurricanes and had a lot of golf planned for his foreseeable future.

Maybe Rutherford knew of a guy.

As reported by DKPittsburghsports.com, Morehouse opened the conversation by saying, "Jim, I need your help. I need a GM, and I could use some advice. I'm looking for someone to come in here with all the talent we've got, all the stars, and get us right again."

As luck would have it, Rutherford knew a guy . . . by the name of Rutherford.

After some early mishaps, GM Jim Rutherford delivered on his pledge to bring the Stanley Cup back to Pittsburgh. *(Chaz Palla)*

BRINGING IT ALL BACK HOME

The Penguins interviewed 22 men for their vacant GM post. They even threw a scare into the fan base by making one of them NBC analyst Pierre McGuire before settling on 65-year-old Jim Rutherford.

It was a homecoming of sorts for Rutherford, a former Penguins goalie. And one thing became immediately clear: he was not afraid to speak his mind.

At his introductory news conference, Rutherford appraised the Penguins this way: "Obviously, they can score in bunches, but based on looking at them from a distance, I don't think they could make the proper adjustments against certain teams."

The masses wanted change.

Jim Rutherford was about to provide it.

● ● ●

Shortly after the hire, Morehouse met a reporter (the one who wrote this book) for lunch and told him he could not believe his luck in landing Rutherford, who was thought to be permanently retired.

The hire had not been met with rave reviews—many believed Rutherford had lost his fastball—but Morehouse was thrilled. He told the reporter he thought Rutherford was one of the two or three best GMs in the game.

"We'll see about that," the reporter thought.

Morehouse, of course, would be proven correct. What he didn't know was that one of Rutherford's greatest assets would be an ability to correct his mistakes. Which meant mistakes lay ahead.

MIKE JOHNSTON

The hockey world looked on curiously when the Penguins hired a junior coach, Mike Johnston, to run their star-centric team.

The experiment lasted just 110 games.

Johnston left with the fourth-best regular-season winning percentage (.611) in Penguins history but one of the quietest tenures.

His playoff record was just 1-4. His 2015-16 team was underachieving at 15-10-3 when he was fired. He couldn't watch the Penguins for two months afterward. He finally tuned in to the Cup Final.

"You want to be there," he told the *Pittsburgh Tribune-Review*. "You want to be part of it and wish you could have been. But on the other side, you say, 'Hey, for those good-character, good-quality guys, I hope they have success.' "

Mike Johnston, seen here with assistant coach Gary Agnew, lasted just 110 games behind the Penguins' bench. *(Pittsburgh Tribune-Review)*

DEMANDING DUMOULIN

Boston College defenseman Brian Dumoulin was hardly the headliner in the Jordan Staal trade of 2012.

Then-Penguins GM Ray Shero agreed to send Staal to Carolina in exchange for Brandon Sutter and the No. 8 pick (which would become Derrick Pouliot). That was clear. The third piece was not.

Then-Carolina GM Jim Rutherford offered his second-round pick. Shero balked. He demanded Dumoulin.

"I remember Jimmy saying, 'Ron Francis loves this kid,' " Shero said. "We thought he could play—but to see him on the top pairing with Kris Letang winning a Cup? Whoa, that's pretty good."

Rutherford thought so, too, and was awfully glad he'd granted Shero's wish.

BAD NEWS BARRAGE

It's hard to believe many teams, in any sport, had a worse year of medical news than the Penguins in 2014 . . .

*In January, defenseman Kris Letang stunningly suffered a stroke.

"It's tough to believe," said Letang, who made a swift recovery. "I'm in the .01 percentage."

*In November, defenseman Olli Maatta underwent surgery for a cancerous tumor in his neck. He recovered but would then endure shoulder surgery and the mumps.

*Less than three weeks after Maatta's operation, forward Pascal Dupuis was diagnosed with a blood clot in his lungs and was declared out for six months.

*Less than a month after that, a league-wide mumps outbreak invaded the locker room, infecting team captain Sidney Crosby, among others.

No, 2014 was not a good year.

TROOPER DUPER

In December of 2013, two days before Christmas, Pascal Dupuis sustained a horrific knee injury, tearing his ACL, MCL, and PCL in a game at Ottawa.

Dupuis refused a stretcher.

"My father had a rule about that: unless both of your legs are broken, you never lay on the ice," Dupuis wrote in the *Players' Tribune*. "You skate off on the good one. So that's what I did."

That kind of fire raged inside Dupuis his whole career. It's what allowed him twice to return from a blood clot in his lung, a complication related to his knee injury.

When the first clot returned, Dupuis kept the frightening symptoms—severe chest pain included—to himself and kept playing. He did not want to give up the game.

As he recalled in *The Players' Tribune*: "I would not recommend this to anyone, but the truth is that I played five more NHL games without ⅓ of a lung."

• • •

Sidney Crosby teared up when Dupuis finally had to hang up his skates early in the 2015-16 season. Teammates adored Dupuis.

So when the Penguins won the Stanley Cup in San Jose on June 12, 2016—seven years to the day of their last title—they made darn sure the man they called "Duper" donned his No. 9 one last time to help them hoist it.

BIG DEAL

Of all the problems that plagued the Penguins during their repeated playoff failures, one stood out: a team-wide allergy to the blue paint in front of the net.

Hence, Jim Rutherford's first big move was to trade for a man hopelessly addicted to blue paint.

Patric Hornqvist patterned his game after fellow Swede Tomas Holmstrom, a legendary net-front menace who'd tortured the Penguins in previous years.

Patric Hornqvist gave the Penguins precisely what they needed: a front-of-the-net warrior for the playoffs. *(Pittsburgh Tribune-Review)*

To get Hornqvist, Rutherford gave up a prolific sniper in James Neal. The trade wasn't overly popular. But Rutherford proved prophetic when he said of Hornqvist: "He'll be good in the playoffs."

In fact, he was great in the playoffs. Hornqvist scored 11 goals in his first 29 postseason games with the Penguins and made many other goals possible (see: Conor Sheary, overtime, Game 2 of Cup Final) by taking a beating right in front of the goalie.

In the blue paint.

SULLIVAN'S TRAVELS

The first time Mike Sullivan stood before his new players, on December 13, 2015, he delivered the truth as he saw it. He'd just been promoted from the team's Wilkes-Barre/Scranton farm club.

"We have some great players in this room," Sullivan said, his booming baritone bouncing off the walls. "Our challenge is to become a great team. It's my responsibility to try to facilitate that process."

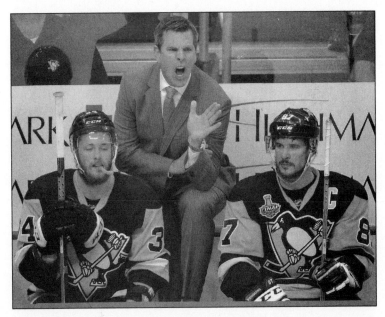

Mike Sullivan gave the Penguins some much-needed direction and a swift kick in the pants after he replaced Mike Johnston during the 2015-16 season. *(Christopher Horner)*

This was a different Mike Sullivan from the one who'd coached his hometown Boston Bruins 13 years earlier. Getting fired four times (three as an assistant) will change a man.

He was wiser. His rough edges were smoothed. But make no mistake: he was still as serious as sin.

One member of the Penguins' organization with insight on the team's new coach was Matt Herr, executive director and general manager of the UPMC Lemieux Sports Complex where the team practiced. Herr had played for Sullivan in the minors a decade earlier.

"At times, he'll chew you a new (rear end), but he was never intimidating to talk to," Herr said. "He coaches the person, not just the player. Guys respect him because he's a former player and has incredible intensity. I'd play for this guy again in a second."

OK, but does the man ever crack a smile?

"I've seen him laugh," Herr insisted. "When he makes the playoffs, you'll see him laugh."

• • •

Sullivan's story played out in eerily similar fashion to Dan Bylsma's. Like Bylsma, Sullivan was promoted from Wilkes-Barre in-season and oversaw a ridiculous hot streak that extended into the playoffs.

Bylsma went 18-3-4 in the regular season, 16-8 in the playoffs. Sullivan went 33-16-5 and 16-8. Both saw their season end in the exact same spot: downtown Pittsburgh.

At a really big parade.

11

STORMIN' BACK

(2015-16)

JUST PLAY

When Mike Sullivan arrived in December of 2015, the Penguins were perceived as a whiny bunch. Referees weren't fond of them. Certain players had a penchant for drama.

Sully changed all that.

He knew the Penguins had come undone in playoffs past. He knew they were seen as fragile and volatile.

The solution?

"Just play."

The Penguins began to live by that motto. It was printed on the backs of T-shirts players wore around the locker room.

Before Game 1 of the Stanley Cup Final, Sullivan delivered a speech built around the "Just Play" theme:

"We can't be off the charts so high that we lose our focus. We need controlled emotion. We need laser focus. Regardless of what happens out there, good or bad, we just play. That's what we've done all season. We just play. OK? That's why it's on the back of your T-shirts, right? Let's play fast. Let's play fearless, and let's have a relentless attack. Let's get Game 1."

They got it: 3-2.

WELCOME MATT

Nobody paid much mind when the Penguins signed 39-year-old Matt Cullen to a one-year, $800,000 deal in the summer of 2015.

Relentlessly upbeat center Matt Cullen provided leadership and clutch all-around play on the Penguins' march to a championship. *(AP Photo/Keith Srakocic, File)*

They sure noticed when the effervescent Cullen lifted the Cup six months later, though. He brought a multitude of skills and experiences to a youthful team.

Cullen's 20-year professional career started with Baltimore of the American Hockey League and wound through Cincinnati, Anaheim, Florida, Carolina, Italy, New York, Ottawa, Minnesota, Nashville, and Pittsburgh.

Wait, Italy?

Cullen played there during the 2004-05 lockout.

"The most unbelievable experience," he said. "My wife (Bridget) and I went, and it was like the Aspen of Italy. It was Cortina, a beautiful little town up in the mountains near Austria. I wouldn't trade that year for anything. The people were awesome. I ate more good food than I could ever hope to again. Whenever I think back, it was like a dream."

THE REVEREND

What were the Penguins thinking? That was the consensus opinion on May 2, 2015, the day the club traded a strapping young defenseman named Simon Despres to Anaheim for a not-so-strapping, not-so-young defenseman named Ben Lovejoy. Even Penguins GM Jim Rutherford soon expressed regret.

But that was before Lovejoy helped the Penguins win the Cup.

Don't think he wasn't keeping score.

While everyone around the team was careful not to mention the words "Stanley" and "Cup" during their 24-game march to a title, Lovejoy let the phrase slip after Game 4 of the conference final, an overtime victory over the Capitals in which he started the play that led to the winning goal.

By this time, Lovejoy—nicknamed "The Reverend" after the "Reverend Lovejoy" character on *The Simpsons*—had established himself in his second Pittsburgh stint as a likable team leader and trustworthy player. He admitted to being acutely aware of the harsh criticism from a year earlier.

It stayed with him as a motivator.

"I'd be lying if I said it didn't," Lovejoy said. "I grew up a die-hard sports fan. I understand the comparisons. [Despres] is a good player. I wish him success. But I would love to be the first one to win the Stanley Cup in that trade."

Nine wins later, The Reverend crossed the finish line.

Simon who?

• • •

Lovejoy wouldn't call Pittsburgh home for long. He parlayed an outstanding playoff into a lucrative free-agent deal with the New Jersey Devils. But as with "The Piece"—Rob Scuderi—from seven years earlier, the understated contributions of "The Reverend" should never be forgotten.

PHIL-ER UP

When a Pittsburgh columnist (the one who wrote this book) suggested the Penguins trade for Toronto Maple Leafs winger Phil Kessel in the summer of 2015, readers rebelled in the comments section.

"Kessel is a head case."

"Kessel is a spoiled little boy."

"And we need a head case because . . ."

Because the Penguins couldn't score in the playoffs anymore, that's why. They once scored all of two goals in an entire series against the Bruins. They needed clutch offense.

The Toronto media had skewered Kessel for his eating habits (too many hot dogs?), his offseason workout habits (too much fishing?), and anything else they could muster.

"I don't know how many times he goes fishing, and I don't care," said Penguins GM Jim Rutherford, "as long as he comes and plays his game."

Kessel played his game in the postseason, ringing up 10 goals and 22 points in 24 games despite playing with a hand injury that would require surgery over the summer.

Phil Kessel, here shown sticking it to San Jose in the Stanley Cup Final, justified GM Jim Rutherford's faith in him with a fabulous playoff. *(Chaz Palla)*

He would schedule the surgery around his fishing trips, of course—and around the day he brought the Cup to a hospital in Toronto.

● ● ●

During the playoffs, Rutherford shot back at Kessel's critics, particularly those based in Toronto.

"For some reason, lots of people don't like Phil Kessel," Rutherford told the *Pittsburgh Trib*. "He's only the best player Toronto had for eight years. He got the blame for everything, which is very unfair."

BEAU KNOWS INJURIES

Nobody, not even Martin Straka, could top Beau Bennett in the category of "Most Injury-Prone Penguin Ever."

The affable Bennett arrived in the NHL with a damaged wrist, the result of a bungled diagnosis. He proceeded to incur injury after

Beau Bennett might have been the worst-luck Penguin since Martin Straka—
and that's saying something. *(AP Photo/Keith Srakocic)*

injury during a star-crossed, four-year Penguins career in which he
appeared in just 129 games. He even hurt himself celebrating a goal.

Knee, wrist, shoulder, ribs.

You name it, Beau hurt it.

Credit him for retaining his sense of humor. After he was traded to New Jersey, Bennett sent Pittsburgh a heartfelt good-bye via social media, thanking "management, coaches, trainers and fans."

He ended the note this way: "P.S. I did not break my thumbs typing this message."

SLAP ME SILLY, SIDNEY!

The zaniest of Mike Lange's newer goal calls, all in the tradition of standards like "Scratch my back with a hacksaw!" has to be the one he busted out for the 2016 Stanley Cup Final.

He used it more than once, most notably on Brian Dumoulin's slap shot in the Game 6 clincher.

"Oh, that makes you want to see a silly seal slide sideways in Sausalito!"

As explained in the new foreword to this book, Lange said the phrase "popped into my brain" in the middle of the night. Some of his other 21st-century calls have different origins.

We'll let him explain . . .

— *Oh, slap me silly, Sidney!* — "My dad used to say, 'Slap me silly.' It made me laugh every time. I just threw a 'Sidney' in there and said, 'Boy, that might work.' "

— *Start frying the jumbo, Homer. Extra crispy please!* — "I just heard somebody say that, believe it or not, and it stuck with me. I stole it as fast as I could and put a little wrinkle in with the, 'Extra crispy please.' "

— *Get that dog off my lawn!* (used on Kris Letang's Cup-winning goal). — "That's one of mine. I think everyone has said that at one time in their life."

— *She wants to sell my monkey!* — "That's an old blues song from the '30s. Tampa Red."

— *Donna needs a donut!* — "That came from the bar at (Pittsburgh restaurant) Tambellini's, during a Christmas party. Somebody was teasing a woman named Donna and said, 'Oh, Donna needs a donut.' "

— *Make me a milkshake, Malkin!* — "That came from a junior reporter, a middle-school student named Dylan Cleland (who interviewed Lange after winning a contest). We're up in the stands, I'm with his parents. I say, 'All right, Dylan, since you know everything about me, why don't you give me a phrase I can use on a broadcast?' He did not hesitate in any way. Right out of nowhere he says, 'Make me a milkshake, Malkin.' I knew right away we had something."

ZATKOFF'S MIRACLE

By the time the Penguins won their 24th and final playoff game, it was easy to forget that a third-string goalie started the run.

With the club facing its playoff nemesis, the New York Rangers, coach Mike Sullivan kept his Game 1 starter a mystery until Jeff Zatkoff stunningly led teammates onto the ice. Neither Marc-Andre Fleury nor Matt Murray was available because of head injuries.

Zatkoff turned back an early Rangers onslaught and made 35 saves in a 5-2 win. His cohorts were thrilled for him.

"The best teammate anybody in this room has ever played with," said defenseman Ben Lovejoy.

Surprise hero Jeff Zatkoff reflects before the biggest game of his life: Game 1 against the Rangers in the 2016 Stanley Cup playoffs. *(Philip G. Pavely)*

• • •

In Columbia, Kentucky, the elder Jeff Zatkoff—"Big Jeff," as the family calls him—watched alone as his son matched saves with Henrik Lundqvist.

Big Jeff pulled on his Penguins No. 37 jersey, the one the team had recently given him on its annual road trip where players are joined by their fathers. Little Jeff told him a night earlier he was starting.

"It was a lot of nerves for Dad from that point on," Big Jeff said. "I wore the jersey for good luck."

Big Jeff was a basketball star at Eastern Michigan, drafted by the Indiana Pacers. Nothing he did on a basketball court, however, could match the excitement of watching his son that night—especially when the crowd started chanting his name as time wound down.

Big Jeff at first thought they were cheering for Patric Hornqvist, who had a hat trick. Then the realization hit.

"Oh my gosh," he said. "I had chills from my neck to my feet."

THE COACH WHO LOST ON PURPOSE

Lou Angotti was a ferociously competitive hockey player. First captain of the Philadelphia Flyers. Played every shift as if it were his last.

So you can imagine it was tough on Angotti years later, as Penguins coach, when he felt compelled to lose on purpose.

Tough? In actuality, it was torturous.

In 1983-84, the Penguins needed to finish last overall in order to secure a once-in-a-lifetime prospect named Mario Lemieux. Then-GM Ed Johnston has never admitted to tanking, although every shred of evidence would indicate that he massaged his roster.

One thing E.J. did not do was tell his coach how to manipulate games. Angotti admitted in a 2016 interview with the *Pittsburgh Trib*, after the Penguins won their fourth Cup, just how far he took it.

"It was tough waking up in the morning," he said. "It was far more strenuous trying to figure out (how to lose) than it would be trying to play a normal game. I remember we got a penalty, and I sent out two players I wouldn't normally put out there. One player yelled to me, 'Louie, what the hell are you doing?'

"If the game started off badly, there wasn't much for me to do. It was the games where we were competitive and looked like we were going to win where I was in position to put us in a position to lose."

Angotti put no blame on his players.

"I can honestly say the players who came to work every day gave all they had," he said. "That was the tough part. I was playing against them. It was me against them. They were trying to win, and I was using them to lose."

The Penguins finished with a league-low 38 points—just three behind the New Jersey Devils—and drafted Lemieux.

By losing, they had won. Angotti never coached another game, at any level, but he felt a sense of pride in having helped to secure the future of the franchise.

EXTRA SAUCE

Uh-oh. That was Andy Saucier's initial thought after he radioed the Penguins' bench early in Game 6 of the Eastern Conference Final at Tampa Bay.

The Penguins were facing elimination. Tampa's Jonathan Drouin had just given his team a 1-0 lead. The crowd was going nuts. The Penguins were in trouble.

Or so it seemed.

In the Penguins' locker room, the man they call "Sauce," the team's video coach, thought he spotted Drouin's skate a few inches offside. He quickly radioed assistant coach Rick Tocchet on the bench. Tocchet relayed the information to coach Mike Sullivan, who asked for a challenge.

Just then, Sauce began to doubt himself.

"There was a little panic," Saucier told the *Pittsburgh Tribune-Review*. "Then they showed a few replays, and we kind of calmed down."

The same could not be said of the crowd. As "Let it Be" rang through the arena, officials reviewed the play and finally waved off the goal, setting off a cascade of boos. The Penguins soon grabbed the lead on their way to a 5-2 victory.

• • •

Who the heck is Andy Saucier? That question emerged in the hours following the Penguins' big win, and it turned out Saucier had deep Penguins ties.

His grandfather Jack Kelley was Penguins president from 1993-98. His uncle Mark Kelley was the Penguins' long-time European scout who advanced to vice president of amateur scouting for the three-time champion Chicago Blackhawks.

"I went to a couple of (Mark's Stanley Cup) parties," Saucier told centralmaine.com, "and was really in awe of the trophy."

Those likely weren't the only interesting parties Saucier attended. His uncle David Kelley (Mark's brother) is an accomplished television writer and producer (*Ally McBeal*) who is married to Michelle Pfeiffer.

MATT MURRAY AVE.

Who would have thought a rookie goalie would have a street named after him before Sidney Crosby would receive such an honor?

It happened.

Murray Avenue, in a part of the city called Squirrel Hill, briefly became "Matt Murray Avenue"—with a real street sign and everything—during the Stanley Cup Final.

"I didn't think it was a real thing," Murray said. "I don't even know where Squirrel Hill is."

Opposing shooters found only dead ends when trying to beat Murray, who replaced an injured Marc-Andre Fleury. His 15 postseason wins made him only the sixth rookie goalie since 1987 to win 10 or more.

While outdueling Henrik Lundqvist and Vezina Trophy winner Braden Holtby on the way to the Final, the 21-year-old Murray

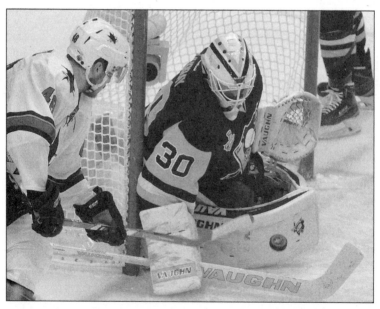

Matt Murray, wearing a mask patterned after that of long-ago Penguins goalie Denis Herron, calmly turned away the San Jose Sharks in the Cup Final. (Christopher Horner)

seemed so preternaturally calm that you half-expected him to break into Zen yoga in his goal crease.

"You almost have to take a step back sometimes," Murray said. "And just relax and take a deep breath and just kind of say, 'Here I am. I'm in the moment.'"

• • •

Further evidence of Murray's groundedness could be found on his mask. On one side was a Dutch flag under the initials of his mother. On the other, a Scottish flag and the initials of his father.

Between them was Thunder Bay's famous landmark, Sleeping Giant, to honor Murray's hometown.

RUST NEVER SLEEPS

Do-or-die games often produce unexpected heroes. Max Talbot was one such hero in 2009.

Bryan Rust was one in 2016.

Rust scored both of the Penguins' goals in Game 7 of the Eastern Conference Final against Tampa Bay. If not for a missed breakaway, he would have been the first rookie in NHL history with a Game 7 hat trick.

"I'm not sure Rusty would have been the guy I would have picked (to be the hero)," coach Mike Sullivan said, "but certainly I love what he brings to this team."

It wasn't Rust's first clutch performance. He had two goals in a series-clinching Game 5 win over the Rangers, and back at Notre Dame he scored in an outdoors game at Fenway Park and in every game of the Irish's playoff series upset of Boston College.

• • •

Rust's older brother Matt was a linemate of Penguins winger Carl Hagelin at Michigan before he spent a year in the Penguins' minor-league system. As children, Matt and Bryan attended speech therapy together to help with their stutters.

"It's not the easiest thing to go through as a kid," Matt told SI.com. "We were always there for each other."

Bryan Rust conjured his best Max Talbot and unexpectedly became a Game 7 hero for the Penguins. *(Christopher Horner)*

Continuing what had become a superstitious habit, Matt watched Game 7 against Tampa Bay on the couch in his Ann Arbor condo, with only a burrito serving as company.

He was connected in spirit to his brother, who would become one of the Penguins' many heroes over the next few weeks.

12

CHAMPIONS AGAIN!

(2015–16 playoffs)

BREATH CHECK

A hilarious mistake led to Phil Kessel's finest moment in front of a microphone.

Shortly after Kessel's maestro performance in Game 3 of the Eastern Conference finals at Tampa Bay, he sat on the bench for an interview with NBC's Pierre McGuire.

First know this: interviews with the ultra-reserved Kessel are usually short and predictable. He answers questions economically and looks to move on. Nothing wrong with that. Some guys just don't like the spotlight.

The interaction was moving along as expected until McGuire posed the following question: "How's your breath?"

What?

Kessel briefly appeared flummoxed before answering: "It's not good, eh?"

McGuire: "No, I meant in terms of conditioning!"

With that, Kessel let out a belly laugh. It was impossible not to laugh along. McGuire, through a poorly worded question, had inadvertently humanized his subject.

Needless to say, Kessel's teammates seized the moment. When he arrived for the game-day skate two days later, he found Listerine and packs of gum in his locker.

SID'S CALLED SHOT

Sidney Crosby has always seen the ice differently than most, but this was ridiculous.

This was Babe Ruth stuff.

Sid didn't call his own shot, mind you, the way legend says Ruth once did. He called somebody else's. Or at least choreographed it.

Flash back to overtime of Game 2 of the Stanley Cup Final. The Penguins were set for an offensive-zone faceoff in the left circle.

Crosby huddled his teammates and drew up the play like a sandlot quarterback. He told them he would win the faceoff (against Joel Ward) back to defenseman Kris Letang.

Crosby ordered Conor Sheary to change his usual routine and line up on the boards, then cut to the slot. San Jose would be concerned about the point shot and move toward Letang, who would slip the puck to Sheary for a wide-open look.

Darned if it didn't happen.

Sheary found a clearing, took a deft pass from Letang, and used a Patric Hornqvist screen to rip a shot past Martin Jones for a 2-1 victory. Crosby watched from the other side of the ice like a proud papa.

He deflected all credit afterward.

"I call 25 faceoffs a game," Crosby said. "So I got 24 wrong tonight."

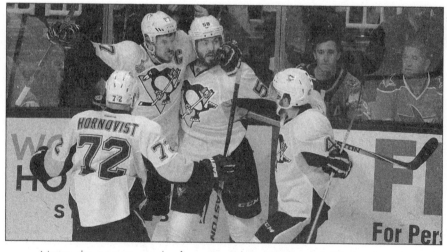

Notice the intensity on the faces as Sidney Crosby and Kris Letang join teammates to celebrate Letang's goal in Game 6 of the Cup Final. It would prove to be the series-winning goal. *(Photo by Chaz Palla)*

His teammates knew better. They swore this was the act of a rare hockey prophet.

"Sid came up to me and told me to line up on the wall," Sheary confirmed. "We hadn't really done that before. He said he would win it back and Letang would find me in the soft area. It worked out perfectly."

OK, since he choreographed every step, did Sid also tell Sheary he would score?

Sheary laughed.

"That's the only thing he left out."

BE LIKE CONOR

Kid gets cut from his high school team, uses the slight as motivation, and launches a lifelong revenge tour.

Sound familiar?

It should. It's the Michael Jordan story.

It's also the Conor Sheary story.

Way back in the fall of 2006, Sheary arrived at prestigious Cushing Academy, a prep school in Ashburnham, Massachusetts, intent on making the varsity as a ninth grader.

His heart raced as he looked at the two rosters on the locker room door after tryouts. Tradition said players on the "A" team got to move their gear into the room right away. Sheary's name wasn't on it. He was listed on the "B" team, essentially the freshmen team.

Legend has it that when Jordan didn't see his name on the varsity list, he went home and cried. Sheary didn't take his cut much better.

"I probably had to hold back some tears," he recalled. "But it was motivation, for sure. It's always motivation when someone tells you you're not good enough."

The man who cut Sheary retained a sense of humor about it. Steve Jacobs, after all, had once cut his own son from the Cushing "A" team. And let's be honest: in Sheary's own words, he was "5 feet tall and like 110 pounds" at the time.

"Maybe I should have kept him, you know?" Jacobs said, laughing. "I didn't always make the wisest decisions, I guess."

• • •

Sheary became an inspiration for male and female hockey players at Cushing. His sister, Courtney, preceded him as a Cushing standout. She later became the girls varsity coach and used her brother as an example.

"He never really had a growth spurt," Courtney recalled. "One of the guys (from admissions) who interviewed Conor tells me he was so little his feet were dangling from the interview chair. It's a bit of an exaggeration, but we talk about Conor as an example of someone who really stuck with it."

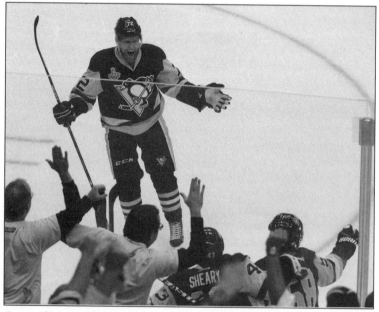

Conor Sheary and Kris Letang await a joyous Patric Hornqvist after Sheary beat the Sharks on Sidney Crosby's "called play" in Game 1 of the Final. (Philip G. Pavely)

BONINO BONINO BONINOOOOO!

When Nick Bonino scored a late tying goal in Game 1 of a first-round series against the Washington Capitals, Punjabi broadcaster Harnarayan Singh sang it loud and clear, eight times in succession like a manic soccer announcer:

"BONINO-BONINO-BONINO-BONINO-BONINO-BONINO-BONINO-BONINOOOOO!"

A star was born.

Not Bonino. Singh.

The call spread like wildfire on social media. It appeared on T-shirts and hats. Penguins coach Mike Sullivan used it during film sessions. Players could do impressions on the spot.

"You'd be amazed at how many times it gets said in this locker room," said defenseman Ben Lovejoy.

Somebody asked Bonino if he used the call as his ringtone.

"I told my family they should get it," he said. "Then they'd know I'm calling."

• • •

Singh, a 31-year-old broadcaster for Hockey Night in Canada's Punjabi edition (Punjabi being a language native to inhabitants of Pakistan and Northern India), got the idea for the call when he accidentally listed Bonino at all three forward positions on his pregame notes.

Colleagues noticed. They jabbed him about the possibility of a Bonino-Bonino-Bonino line taking the ice.

The call was so popular that the Penguins invited Singh—who called games from a studio in Vancouver—to speak at their Stanley Cup parade.

"Until we got to Pittsburgh," Singh said, "we didn't realize it was that big."

CRAZY COINCIDENCE

Jeff Zatkoff shocked the hockey world in the first game of the playoffs, a game in which he saved 35 of 37 shots against the New York Rangers. That same night, Zatkoff's spiritual predecessor received a text just before faceoff.

Frank Pietrangelo was not aware that April 13, 2016, happened to be the 25th anniversary of "The Save," his miracle stop on Peter Stastny in the 1991 playoffs, until his daughter Paige texted him at home in Niagara Falls, Ontario.

"All of a sudden I was hearing from people all over the states, texting and Facebooking and everything else," Pietrangelo said. "And then the game goes that way. What are the chances of that?"

Not good.

Not good at all.

MINUTE MAN

Kris Letang made a pretty solid case for the Conn Smythe Trophy. Letang rang up seven 30-minute games in the postseason. He had 15 points in 23 games. He played against the other team's best players.

Oh, and he scored an amazing Cup-winning goal.

Halfway through the second period of Game 6, just after San Jose tied the score 1-1, Letang faked a shot at the left point, went to his backhand, and spun around Joe Pavelski.

Letang pulled the puck back from another Shark and wheeled behind the net before throwing it into the slot.

As players scrambled for possession, Letang positioned himself at the bottom of the far circle. He then took a brilliant pass from Sidney Crosby and fired the puck from a harsh angle past Martin Jones.

"We're so spoiled by him." Penguins assistant Sergei Gonchar told the *Pittsburgh Tribune-Review*. "Not just the fans but teammates and coaches."

DELAYED GRATIFICATION

Nobody, not even ancient Ed Johnston, had seen anything like this.

While trying to protect a third-period lead in Game 6 against the Capitals, the Penguins, in the span of 2 minutes, 2 seconds, took three delay-of-game penalties for clearing the puck over the glass.

Chris Kunitz, Nick Bonino, and Ian Cole all put pucks out of play—Bonino's coming on a ridiculously unlucky clearing attempt.

The power plays helped Washington wipe out a 3-0 lead and force overtime, but the Penguins were as calm as could be in their dressing room. They won it on Bonino's goal at 6:32 of overtime, setting off a wild celebration at Consol Energy Center.

"The first half of the season," defenseman Ben Lovejoy said, "the Penguins would have found a way to lose that game."

NICK OF TIME

Nobody had Nick Bonino pegged for playoff stardom. Perhaps we should have known better. Bonino developed a penchant for scoring big goals long before he arrived in Pittsburgh.

Nick Bonino-Bonino-Boninooooo! scores the series-clinching overtime goal against the Washington Capitals. *(Pittsburgh Tribune-Review)*

Back in high school, he scored in double overtime to win the 2005 Connecticut state championship.

In college, he scored the tying goal with 17.4 seconds left in regulation in Boston University's comeback win over Miami of Ohio in the 2009 NCAA Frozen Four championship game.

In the NHL, playing for Anaheim, he scored an overtime series-winner against Dallas in 2014.

Throw in his four postseason goals in 2016, including the one that eliminated the Washington Capitals, and you get this: five of his 12 playoff goals have been game-winners, the last four of coming in the final three minutes of regulation or overtime.

Nick of time, indeed.

• • •

Bonino had good reason for missing several practices in the play-offs: he developed a fever on account of an elbow infection and needed antibiotics and IV fluids to get through.

Doctors threatened to make Bonino sit if his temperature rose to 101 degrees.

"It was dicey, but it was up and down," he said. "I was quarantined. I was in the hotel. I wasn't even living at home because they didn't want me around (5-month-old daughter Maisie). It was a weird time. But it was worth it to win."

• • •

Showtime cameras caught the following interaction between Nick Bonino and coach Mike Sullivan as the Penguins celebrated on the ice after winning the Cup.

Sullivan: "You played unbelievable."

Bonino: "You coached pretty good, too."

Sullivan: "Thanks, pal."

MOJO GIFTS

Anyone who knows hockey players knows they can be incredibly superstitious.

Their significant others can be that way, too.

Leslie Rutherford, wife of general manager Jim Rutherford, started a tradition of handing out "mojo gifts" for playoff games when the couple was in Carolina and the Hurricanes won the Cup.

As chronicled by Michelle Crechiolo of the Penguins' media team, Leslie continued her tradition in Pittsburgh. She gave a gift to each player's significant other for good luck and attached "an inspirational quote to each one."

Some nights, Crechiolo wrote, Leslie would stay up until 4 a.m. finishing the gifts, all tailored to the situation at hand.

After a loss to San Jose in the Cup Final, for example, she distributed hand towels monogrammed with every player's number on it and a note attached: "Don't throw in your towels yet."

Leslie also found a hot sauce in San Jose named "shark repellant" and had bottles shipped across the country in time for a game.

Did it help the Penguins win?

It surely didn't hurt.

THE HBK LINE

Like so many great sports stories, this one was born of accident.

The Penguins were desperately fighting for a playoff spot when Evgeni Malkin went down with a significant elbow injury late in the season in Columbus.

Instead of ruining their hopes, the injury helped catapult them all the way to the Stanley Cup.

Coach Mike Sullivan decided to try Nick Bonino in Malkin's place between Carl Hagelin and Phil Kessel. It proved to be an inspired choice, though Sullivan admitted he could not have foreseen the explosive chemical reaction.

The trio racked up 20 goals and 56 points in 24 playoff games and earned a wonderful nickname along the way: The HBK Line, as in Hagelin, Bonino, Kessel. It played on the nickname of a famous pro wrestler named Shawn Michaels, a.k.a. the "Heartbreak Kid."

The HBK Line—Carl Hagelin, Nick Bonino, and Phil Kessel—struck this pose often during the spring of 2016. *(Christopher Horner)*

The line was a testament to the fine work of GM Jim Rutherford. All three players were acquired in trades.

Malkin returned to help the Penguins win it all. But would they have won if he hadn't temporarily left the lineup?

Would Sullivan have tried Bonino in that spot?

"That's a tough question to answer," Sullivan said. "I'm not sure how likely I would have been to try that combination."

DALEY'S COMET

He didn't make it out of the playoffs in one piece, but, man, did Trevor Daley make his contribution count.

If a single snapshot could represent the Penguins' singleness of purpose, it might be Daley—after breaking his ankle in a corner collision in Game 4 at Tampa Bay—crawling into the danger area in front of his goaltender and positioning himself on all fours until the whistle blew.

Then there was his performance in Game 4 against Washington. Playing without suspended No. 1 defenseman Kris Letang, the Penguins desperately needed someone to absorb his minutes if not approximate his elite production.

Daley did both. He played 28 minutes and 41 seconds, scored a goal, and finished plus-3.

"I kind of knew what the situation was going to be like," Daley said. "Every play matters."

PRIVATE VIEWING

At the Penguins' Stanley Cup parade, Mike Lange told the following story about team captain Sidney Crosby:

"When we left the building in San Jose the other night, there were some stragglers around, and I was one of them. The bus had come back from the hotel to pick us up. A few players were there, and the last one to come to the bus, carrying the Cup, was Sidney Crosby.

"As we got to the bus, you could hear, up a ramp in San Jose, fans chanting, 'Let's go Pens! Let's go Pens!' Sid walked right by that bus, took the Cup, went up the ramp, and held it up—and they were thrilled to death. That's your captain. He sees it. He gets it. And that's why you've got a championship team this year."

Sidney Crosby kisses the Stanley Cup during the parade as jubilant fans cheer from the street—and from a multilevel parking garage. *(Photo by Justin Merriman)*

FIRST WITH THE CUP

Whenever a team wins the Cup, intrigue sets in: Who will the team captain hand the Cup to first?

In the Penguins' case, Sidney Crosby had no doubt. It would be injured defenseman Trevor Daley, who had confided in Crosby that his mother, Trudy, was suffering from cancer and wanted to see her son lift the Stanley Cup.

"That kind of stuck with me after he told me that," Crosby said.

Daley was touched.

"It was pretty special," he said. "[Crosby] is a great player, but he's an even better person. He's a special guy."

Those who'd played with Daley over his 838 NHL games felt the same way about him.

Hall of Famer Mike Modano, who teamed with Daley in Dallas, tweeted the following while watching the Penguins celebrate: "That's how great a teammate everyone thinks Trevor Daley is: 1st guy to get the Cup from Crosby."

GET IN THE FAST LANE, GRANDMA!

As the Penguins readied to leap over the boards and celebrate their championship, Mike Lange described the scene:

"Four seconds to go, and the Penguins have jumped over the boards. . . . It's over! Get in the fast lane, Grandma, the Bingo game is ready to roll! The 2016 Stanley Cup champions. The Pittsburgh Penguins!"

• • •

As he observed, for the fourth time in his career, the Penguins parading the Cup around somebody else's ice, Lange called it this way: "These players, this is something they will never, ever forget. The bond between them is something you have to experience to really understand. This will carry the rest of their lives."

Medical issues forced the irrepressible Pascal Dupuis to retire during the season, but his teammates made sure he took a turn with the Cup. *(Photo by Chaz Palla)*

LOVE A PARADE

Despite an overnight rain that fell like ticker tape, some fans arrived 12 hours early for the Penguins' 11:30 a.m. Stanley Cup parade.

The PPG Towers provide a dramatic backdrop as 400,000 fans gather downtown to fete their Stanley Cup champion Penguins. *(Photo by Stephanie Strasburg, Tribune-Review)*

They would soon be joined by about 400,000 of their closest friends.

That number was a 25,000-person increase on the 2009 parade. And just like in '09, fans lined the streets 10-20 deep in parts and filled multilevel parking garages. One group even stood on scaffolding to get a glimpse of players in pickup trucks, convertibles, and even amphibious duck boats.

Coach Mike Sullivan thanked the fans and extended an invitation.

"We know we couldn't have done it without you," he said. "And we know you're going to be there moving forward.

"All I say is, 'Let's do this again next year.'"

REGAL PRESENCE Jack Riley, here wearing a jacket issued during the team's inaugural season of 1967-68, was the Penguins' original general manager and for decades a treasured presence in the press box. He passed away at age 97 on July 14, 2016—barely a month after the Penguins won their fourth Stanley Cup.

Jack was a humble man who lent his time and expertise to anyone who needed it, including the author of this book, which would not have been possible without him. After his wife died in 1988, Jack lived with his daughter Barbara in the South Hills. He had hoped to live to 100.

"I know the numbers aren't there," he said in 2012, at age 93. "At the same time, who knows? I've been pretty lucky so far."

No, Jack. We were the lucky ones. Rest in peace. (James M. Kubus)